How I Mastered My Fear of Public Speaking

ELMER WHEELER

Chosen "Most Popular Speaker"
by poll of 500 business clubs

GRAMERCY PUBLISHING COMPANY
New York

To BETH

Contents

CONTENTS

Foreword

WHY WRITE A BOOK ON PUBLIC SPEAKING?

True, there's no shortage of literature on the subject. There are practical books, theoretical books, books of jokes, Bible quotations, epigrams, how-to-do-it books and you-can-do-it-if-you-try books. Why do I add my booming voice to the chorus? For a number of reasons, all simple.

Nature never intended me to be a speaker. A born speaker should have poise and confidence. He should have a magnetic personality, a flexible and appealing voice. He should command respect and admiration.

As a young man, I was remarkable for the complete lack of all these qualities. I was painfully shy. Words stuck in my throat. People frightened me. Even my mother would have laughed at the idea of Elmer speaking before a group of people.

But I did become a speaker. In the process, I was forced

to learn many things about myself and the art of influencing others. I've since discovered that the fear of getting up before an audience strikes terror into many a brave heart. Perhaps my experiences in overcoming this dread of audiences will be helpful to others. With this hope in mind, I've tried to describe as clearly as I can the baseless fears I had, and the methods I used to master them.

The first time I got up to "say a few words" I was beseiged by every fear known to man. I was certain I'd forget everything I planned to say. My mind would go blank. My voice would crack. No one would pay attention. People would laugh at me and make wisecracks. Everyone would walk out.

To my surprise, none of these calamities happened. I asked myself why. The answer hit me with such impact that I've never forgotten it. The talk went over because I had something unusual to say that they wanted very much to hear. And because I believed so deeply in the value of my suggestions that they caught my enthusiasm.

They didn't listen because I was a polished speaker. I was light years away from that. They weren't held by my captivating voice. At the time, it was high-pitched and colorless. It wasn't my dramatic personality, my flawless diction or my use of showmanship that put me over. I had none of these working for me.

Then and there, I learned a lesson I've used ever since. People want to hear something that will help, instruct or entertain them and the speaker's enthusiasm is vital in getting the talk across.

Of course, as speech followed speech, I picked up many tricks of the trade. I learned how to get the most from my voice, how to dramatize points, when and how to inject humor, how to squelch troublemakers, how to handle a chicken dinner with a minimum of fuss and muss. In the pages that follow I've set down all the speaking "tricks" I've learned through experience and picked up from successful speakers.

Speaking has been very good to me. It has helped me to develop from a shy, retiring stay-at-home into a guy who enjoys people and gets more fun out of life. It's helped me spread my "sizzle" gospel clear across the United States and Canada. Now, Uncle Sam is sending me abroad to tell my story to Army officials overseas. I've delivered one of my speeches six thousand times and people are still asking to hear it.

Possibly you have no desire to be a paid speaker. But whatever your work or way of life, I'm convinced that the ability to stand on your feet and speak intelligently is a vital one.

You will find that this is no standard textbook. It's a purely personal story. It tells what I felt, what I learned and how I developed as a speaker. Much of what I learned was by trial and error. Many early mistakes taught me costly but profitable lessons. Perhaps, by reading my story, you will be saved from making some of the avoidable mistakes I made.

I'm convinced, however, of one thing. Anyone can learn

to speak well in public. Not everyone can be a Jessel, a Hershfield, or a Bob Hope; but everyone can learn to put his ideas and himself across before any group. I can't state this too strongly. It's one thing I know. I know because I've had the amazing experience myself.

Some of the suggestions you'll come across in the book may strike you as unusual, unconventional. All I can say in defense is that all the ideas set down have been helpful to me. I believe they can be helpful to you, too.

For the past ten years I have been writing a newspaper column called "Success Secrets," based on interviews with people who have become famous. I ask them what advice, suggestions or magic formulas they have to offer the world as secrets of their success. So far I have written up some 1,000 men and women, most of whom became millionaires financially as well as millionaires in health and happiness.

One day I decided to examine all the advice, rules and formulas these people told me they used to become successful, to see if I couldn't find a pattern of success that anyone could use.

Believe it or not, I found such a pattern—a formula that you can use to become a success in talking with people.

In this book you will find little discussion of grammar, usage, correct English. I'm more than content to leave this field to the language experts.

If you've happened to hear me speak, you may even have noted a grammatical peccadillo here and there. No disrespect to our beautifully expressive language is intended. Words are an important tool in the expression of ideas but not a substitute for them.

You will find, throughout this book, that the emphasis is on how to get your ideas across to others—not how to win compliments on your speaking ability. Give your audience ideas they can use, information they need. This is the formula that works best for me and will for you too, I believe.

Few assets are more valuable than the ability to express your ideas before a conference group, a luncheon or a meeting. It's important to get ideas. It's even more important to have them acted on. There's nothing so dead as an idea sitting in someone's outgoing basket. Granted it takes effort to face a group or an audience. It takes study to improve your ability to sell your ideas. However, the effort and study can be a wonderful investment in your future.

Public speaking has provided me with some of the pleasantest experiences and associations of my life. I've often had the thrill of watching an entire auidence spark to my ideas. In this book, I've tried to convey my enthusiasm for speaking and I've tried to set down every useful fact I've picked up on this vital art. If others can benefit from my experience, my hopes for this book will be fulfilled.

E.W.

1

I Was a Rank Dud as a Conversationalist

Strange as it may seem, as a young newspaperman I always feared people. I lost not only friends, money and reputation because of my failing, but I started to lose my health as well.

I just couldn't carry on a conversation. Not only with crowds of people, mind you, but even with a few friends gathered in a friendly den, at a noonday luncheon, or at a patio party.

I was always the little fellow you saw sucking his pipe as he sat by himself, alone, in the back of the room, the Pullman, the plane. Always away from people who might want to pass the friendly time of day with me and frighten me to death.

I actually got sick when, at sales meetings or service-club dinners, someone would say, "Elmer, let's hear your ideas." I had ideas to give, but they stuck in my throat. I could never, in those days, stand up and look at a group of faces staring silently at me, waiting for me to say something.

I had one virtue, though. I listened well to others. People liked me as an audience. Perhaps that is the only thing I did right in those days.

But as a conversationalist I was a failure.

When my editor called me into his office to talk things over, I shook in my boots. I always had to lean on his desk, or sit down to cover up my weakness. I'd have to button and unbutton my coat, adjust my tie eternally. I'd turn red in the face, stammer, gulp. I'd lose my voice and my prestige all at the same time.

No wonder I didn't progress very far in the business world.

My inability to hobnob with people soon gave me complexes. I developed a real couch case of inferiorities, and good assignments passed me by. The editor would send me to a game or a big affair where all I had to do was sit quietly in buried silence in the back row and report what I saw and heard. I never received an important assignment to interview anyone.

Why send Elmer out to interview some personality, they reasoned, when he would perhaps have epilepsy just knocking on a hotel door and saying, "I'm from the press."

It is no disgrace to be tongue-tied at times. But people are more apt to send the glib person with a ready-made bon mot always on his lips than the shy one who finds it difficult to say the right words.

2

Don't mistake me. I was not a lonely fellow. By that I mean many others sat quietly with me on the back benches of life. I had lots of company on the sidelines of success. I wasn't lonely, just frustrated.

I tried to help my backwardness, my inferiority complexes, my anxieties in meeting people by taking public-speaking courses. I learned all the techniques and arts of winning an audience, but I failed to learn the one thing back seaters need most of all. That was: *how to overcome the fear of meeting people.* No one ever taught me how to overcome this handicap. I learned when to raise my hand in dramatic platform gesture, and when to raise the glass of water—but I never learned how to raise my spirit!

I was never taught the fundamentals of overcoming stage fright, tension and worry about meeting people, especially strangers.

As long as times were prosperous I found no real reason why I needed to become a front-parlor conversationalist, let alone one who could stand at ease at a sales meeting or a Jaycee luncheon and speak. I had no fear of losing my job, just fear of having to talk to people.

Then came the Great Depression.

I was with the Baltimore *News* and Erwin Huber was my boss. He was a gracious and kindly soul. A great speaker himself. A commander of sales groups. A leader in civic projects. His importance as sales head of the newspaper reflected his ability to meet people and hold their interest.

3

Erwin always had something of value and interest to say to people. I admired him greatly. I wanted so much to be like Erwin.

One day he told me the situation was such that reporters were not indispensable any more, but that, if I would get into the sales end of the newspaper business and sell ads to merchants, he could afford to keep me on.

I died a thousand and one deaths at the thought of going out into the cold streets filled with strangers and talking with tough merchants about spending money for advertisements in my newspaper.

I froze to the office chair when Erwin suggested this. What unfroze me was the thought that has been perhaps the foremost motivator of men—the thought of being hungry and lonesome and without a job. I decided then and there to become a salesman if it killed me, and it almost did until I found the secret of how to meet people and win them to my way of thinking.

Going into selling was the greatest single move I ever made. And it took a vision of hunger to bring about this decision.

The assignment was selling space to the stores and speaking to salespeople on how to sell customers. It was the beginning of a brand-new technique in newspaper selling. The idea was to persuade a merchant to run an ad, then to coach his salespeople with ideas of what to say and when to say it to sell customers. In this way the newspaper ads

4

would have greater pulling power.

Now if you can picture a shy fellow, always hiding behind the fellow in front of him at meetings or parties, suddenly having to go out and rap on doors to sell advertising space, then you see me.

I died a thousand and one deaths thinking about it. I was heartbroken, discouraged, scared to death. I planned to quit the job when the time came for a decision on Friday of that week.

On Thursday night I found myself walking down Charles Street on my way home after work. I became aware of the sudden influx of apple vendors, that army of unemployed that lined the streets at this period in American history.

"How about an apple?" one after another would ask, and I'd shrug "No."

Then an idea hit me. I looked squarely into the face of an apple merchant. He was a vet, too. A fierce-looking chap with a sign that said, I FOUGHT FOR YOU—NOW YOU BUY APPLES FROM ME.

Something hit me. Maybe it was the idea of my being in his place. Maybe the thought of hunger. I don't know, but I got a brain wave. Why not teach this guy the right words to say?

I mustered up courage and said to him, "Here, let me tell you how to sell twice as many apples." He glared at me; then became suddenly interested.

I said: "First, make sure those finger-marked apples are

5

shiny. Use some tissue and keep shining each apple as customers walk by. When one gets close to you hold the apple up and say, 'They are cool and fresh from the apple orchards of New York State—ten cents.' "

If there are any miracles that change a person's life, this was one of them! I had suddenly forgotten my backwardness, my timidity, and had actually accosted a stranger on the street to give him words to sell apples.

The fellow must have been taken by my boldness, for he obeyed me. He wiped off an apple, held it up to a customer and said, "They are cool and fresh from the apple orchards of New York State—ten cents." The customer paused. Then he took out a dime and bought an apple. The vet brightened up. He was a newborn man, a salesman now. He smiled thanks to me as I walked down the street, reborn myself.

I am always amazed at the bedside confessions of famous people (usually with press agent on hand) who come up with a single-sentence formula of how they raised themselves from failure to success. "I just worked, sir, worked hard and long," is about all they have to say.

Always my reportorial instincts tell me that this "formula" they "reveal" is nothing other than common sense, a will to succeed, and a definite pattern to follow—plus, of course, a great motivator to get them started.

As I look back at nineteen years of walking uphill, I doubt that I can summarize in one sentence how I went from a tongue-tied kid to the winner of an Oscar, no less, in public speaking.

I do know that a person who is interesting and can express himself well will go farther up the ladder of prosperity, and faster too, than the person who can't get his ideas into words and in a manner that holds the attention of others.

It took an apple and a depression to transform me from an introvert into one who had lost all fear of meeting people. And each time the hotel manager sends me a basket of fruit, which they frequently do for guest speakers in their hotels, I always take out the apple and put it in full view on my dresser. It has become a symbol of my victory over shyness.

It was a great transformation for me, from an introvert reporter into an extrovert speaker. So when the publisher of this book came to me and asked me to put on paper, in great detail, all the rules and trade secrets I have found in nineteen years of speaking, I leaped at the opportunity.

First, it gave me a chance to write. I like writing. Second, it gave me a way to help others in need of what I had discovered in overcoming my own fears, anxieties and worries about meeting people and talking with them. I want others to overcome this weakness that plagued me for years, holding back my progress, keeping me in the stag lines of life.

I want too to tell you about the great pleasures I have had since I learned how to whip worry and gain the respect of others.

For who doesn't welcome that fine feeling you get when

you enter a room filled with friendly folks who know you as an interesting talker, or when a roomful of people suddenly becomes silent as you stand up on a podium to talk to them!

Is there a single person who wouldn't give much to enjoy that finest of all exhilarating experiences, that of holding the attention and interest of one or one thousand people? It's a great experience. An exciting adventure.

2

My Career as Public Speaker Begins

I had given the apple vendor courage—and he had given me back courage.

I set out that Friday morning, a new Elmer, a man with words that make people buy, prepared to teach the clerks how to sell my readers when they responded to the store's ads.

Let it be said that the store owners looked at me in amazement when I told them my plans. They knew me as a writer, not a "sales expert," and all were dubious.

Business was pretty bad so I guess they figured, since it cost them nothing, they'd let Elmer give his ideas a whirl.

I used my apple experience as my first example to the salespeople of what can happen when you say the right words to customers. I was, at last, talking in public!

What is more, I liked the idea of seeing faces brighten up when I told my vet story. I had a good audience of interested people, for they too were worried about their futures and if I could show them how to make more sales, they'd listen.

My story was true. It also sounded true—for didn't these people actually see living proof of it each time they went out in the streets!

From this experience, I learned my first important lesson: *Talk about what you know best—your own personal experiences!* If I had been forced to manufacture a story, or repeat one that someone told me, the effect on my audience might have been one of disbelief. I might perhaps have been so discouraged as never to try to speak again in public. But my story was believable and I had proof.

Therefore, the first big rule in holding the interest of others, whether on a patio or a platform, is to sound sincere and believable and the trick in accomplishing this is to tell a true personal experience.

I began to practice this first rule in speaking. I used the apple story until everyone in town had heard it, then I began to tell other first-person stories of my experiences in the stores.

I can remember helping the May store of Baltimore sell out of white shirts for the first time in its history when I had the salespeople hold up a shirt, tug on a button and say: "It won't pop off in the wringer!"

There were some ten things you could say to a busy shop-

10

per looking at shirts, but once you told her the buttons wouldn't pop off, and she visualized no need for constant sewing—that sold her.

When Arrow Shirts heard how this simple selling sentence was selling so many shirts at the May store, they asked permission to make it a part of their national advertising.

I found other ways to use stories based on my personal experience, such as increasing sales of white shoe polish to women buying white shoes at the Hecht Company by 300 per cent by having the sales clerk say, "It won't rub off!"

W. T. Grant's stores sold thirty million square clothespins, nation-wide, with one of my "magic phrases": "It won't roll when dropped—look!"

"How'd you like to cut your shaving time in half, sir?" doubled the sale of Barbasol in the Sears' stores.

Indeed, I had hit upon the first big secret of holding an audience—and that is merely to tell personal experiences.

The person fresh from Europe stands up at a chamber meeting and tells of his fun, pleasures and adventures abroad, and holds the full and rapt attention of an audience not privileged to have been on the trip. A housewife tells her bridge club about her experiences growing a new flower, and her listeners are all eyes and ears. If she tried to explain the political situation, a subject remote to her experience, she'd be called a bore.

We are all experts of some sort in our "fields of daily endeavor." Maybe you have a green thumb, or a pie hand;

11

maybe you have a hobby in the cellar, or make a reading study of TV repair or some subject where your personal experiences might interest others.

I don't mean a housewife must become an expert in paperhanging to hold the attention of her bridge partners, or that a man must take up landscape painting to find interesting things to say.

I don't mean, either, as you'll find out in subsequent rules, that you should be egotistical, talking about yourself until others want to scream. "Let me tell you what happened to me the other day . . ." stops all conversation, and gives you the full attention of everyone.

The reason why talking about your own firsthand experiences holds attention is that you know them best of all, you become enthusiastic about your own experiences, and you literally compel attention with the strength of your story. This feeling of confidence that you get bolsters you, and keeps you going. It overcomes fear, for you can't fear the things you know best.

If you are one of the great horde of tongue-tied, learn the great rule of loosening yourself up by telling first-person stories, until you have overcome this fear and are ready to go on to other rules and tricks of the platform for holding interest.

One big error in giving a talk is to speak on subjects others know better than you do. I would hesitate, for example, to tell a group of dentists how to clean a tooth and put in a filling. However, if I were to tell them my experiences in a dental office, and my recommendations for handling patients, then perhaps they'd sit up and listen to this "typical patient" and his ideas.

So I found myself speaking in public. Not a public speaker, mind you, but a fellow just telling his own experience, namely, a story of an apple and an apple vendor.

It wasn't long, as I said, before I found myself broadening my experiences to include a wider range of subjects, and I was becoming a regular Monday morning visitor at such stores as People's Drugs, the May Company, Hutzler's, the Hecht and the Hub stores and others. In fact, Erwin Huber had to start merchandising my speaking time. That was certainly a great step from the day three months before when he had told me to go out and meet and talk to people— or get fired.

I had used my personal-experience technique to start up the first rung on the ladder to speaking success. What is more important, I saw my work advising salespeople what to say to sell more result in great sales gains for the stores and greater happiness for their employees.

If one could be shown that a certain item "saved costly repairs" or "made two cups instead of one," that was certainly doing people a good deed and at the same time bringing the salespeople a better income. Not to mention the fact that my newspaper had, for the first time in history,

13

secured more advertising linage than our competitor, the famed Baltimore *Sun*.

Our principle of telling salespeople the right words to use on our readers who came in response to the ads, brought our paper greater pulling power. Everybody was happy.

Me, especially—for I got a raise!

3

How I Flunked My Way to Success

To dramatize the fact that I was a shy guy, lacking in courage to stand up even in a classroom to tell about Gaul being so divided, let me say that it wasn't long before my Baltimore success got me a story in a magazine that I cherish dearly.

Believe it or not, *Your Life* magazine wrote an article about me called, "He Flunked His Way to Success!"

Now I consider this one of the greatest compliments in my life, that a national magazine should "find" Elmer, tell his story, and use it as inspiration to others who had also failed in early life to learn how to meet people and carry on a conversation.

Years later, when I was given the first "Oscar" in public speaking, I became convinced that anyone with a will to do so can achieve success in the field of speaking in public. No one was lower on the Totem Pole of Success than I was. No one could have sunk much lower than to be nearly fired, not for lack of ability, but because he could not express himself to others. This is perhaps why the magazine said I flunked my way to success.

Indeed, my report cards always showed the lowest grades in public speaking, even though they were average in human relations and English literature.

If I can do it—so can you.

My rise as a "public" speaker was in direct ratio to my ability to talk about the thing I knew best, how to sell, along with an understanding of the lives of salespeople, their problems, daydreams and castles in Spain.

I could, at last, talk to them in their own language and this led to my second rule in winning people: *Talk to others in their own language!* I don't mean that you should talk Polish to a Pole or Chinese to a Chinese, but if you talk about Polish sausage to a Chinese, you are not going to get much attention.

By this I mean they understand you best in New Castle when you talk about coal, and in Tulsa when you talk oil.

One day the training director of the Stewart Company in Baltimore asked me, "How come you claim these words of yours make people buy?"

I told her they were "Tested Selling Sentences"—that they were, in the lingo of the trade, sentences tested to make people buy faster, more often and more surely.

16

From that day on, the era of "Tested Selling Sentences" sprang up nation-wide, for I had hit upon an idea, new in retailing, of using at sales counters sentences as thoroughly tested as the advertising copy or the merchandise itself.

I had begun to find my stride. For as "Tested Selling Sentences" were found to be effective behind the counters, makers came to me for permission to use them all over the country.

One day a real big success came to me. I was invited to Johns Hopkins University, to tell my story to the professors of psychology, headed by Dr. Knight Dunlap. He offered to test my sentences on a device then called the psychogalvano-meter, which became the Lie Detector we know today. The idea was for me to speak my sentences to a "customer" hooked up to the instrument, and as she reacted inwardly, we would find the words which made her respond best. We'd find the exact "Tested Selling Sentence."

My stock in trade went sky-high as this story went around the country—that is, until one day the idea backfired on me.

Macy's, the great New York department store, heard of the work of this young fellow in Baltimore. They invited me to tell my story before their department heads. I was in all my glory. The Big Town had discovered me.

I failed to realize that I was not ripe for the big city, for my success in Baltimore had gone to my head. I went to Macy's.

Erwin Huber was elated to think "his young man" was being called to New York to tell his story. Permission was quickly granted. So I prepared a lot of charts and graphs of my work. I planned to discuss most fully the psychogalvanometer and its tests. I must have looked like something out of the General Electric laboratories when I arrived at the great store.

I stood up before my Macy audience and started to talk. I saw a room filled with strange faces. Cold faces. Faces willing to listen but mirroring skepticism. I found my old bogieman back with me. I became as tongue-tied as ever. You see, I had violated the very rules that had made me a success.

I held up a chart and tried to explain something about which I knew little, the psychogalvanometer. The charts quivered. I quivered. I even found it hard to say "psychogalvanometer" or my pet phrase, "Tested Selling Sentences."

When I sat down after trying to be a young scientist of words, having failed to explain the workings of the instrument in language the store folks could comprehend, I got no more than faint applause.

On the train back to Baltimore I analyzed my errors. I had failed because I had not told my own experiences. How different it would have been if I had started off by saying, "Let me tell you an experience I had in the stores of Baltimore. . . ."

I had tried to flaunt my pseudo knowledge of the psychogalvanometer, instead of talking about the things I knew best.

18

4

How a Mirror Showed Me a Simple Secret

I arrived in Baltimore some five hours later, determined to get back to solid earth. I had learned a lesson and that was to practice what you preach. For how different my applause at Macy's would have been if I had only told how the Baltimore stores were using my "Tested Selling Sentences" methods.

It was a lucky bit of analysis for me, because years later the very same Macy store invited me back again. This time I started off, "Let me tell you an experience I had that started a new trend in selling in Baltimore."

I quickly gulped down my pride when I got back to the friendly stores of old Baltimore, and started my rounds.

But the Big Town urge was still inside me. I had tasted just enough local success to want to hit New York and win it over as I had done with Baltimore.

19

I was now determined not to be an average, run-of-the-mill speaker. I even daydreamed about being a Billy Sunday or another Dr. Russel Conwell, and I guess these castles in Spain kept me going.

I would stand in front of mirrors and watch my delivery. I would ask everybody for ideas for improvement.

It was good training, I found quickly, to give my speech before a mirror. Here I saw myself as others were seeing me, and I learned a lot.

I saw mistakes I was making in facial gestures, in dress, in actions. I often felt disgusted with myself, for the mirror is honest and tells the truth. One day I noticed that my necktie was so loud I could hardly see my face, so I started wearing a more conservative tie. Then I decided upon a bow tie so that the white of my shirt would highlight my face even more. I practiced, for only by practice could I improve.

At times I found my breath was in my throat, as I became enthusiastic and took a deep breath. One day I was told to breathe from the diaphragm.

It took several weeks before it became a normal thing with me, but it sure kept the wind in my chest to sound off with, rather than in my throat to choke me.

As I look back at those first five years of struggling to be a success on the platform, I'd say here is a third great rule for learning the art of speaking in public: *Make daily and excellent use of your mirror.*

One day I noticed in the mirror that my arm movements

were short and stilted. I realized that when you are in front of a large group, arms stretched their full length seem normal. Note this on a political platform. The speaker who stretches his arms their full length seems normal. While the one with short, choppy arm movements looks weak and lacking in confidence.

I began to use free, natural arm movements. Even in small gatherings I find I can hold attention with good arm gestures. It is a trick for all to use in holding the attention of one or a thousand listeners.

The same rules apply, on the whole, in talking to a group around a swimming pool as before a meeting of the Kiwanis Club.

I have heard many people say, "I can get across with my friends, but the minute I get on the platform, I am overcome with fear. Why?"

I believe the "why" is that you fail to realize that one hundred people are merely one person times the rest; that what interests one person when you speak in the patio will interest the ninety-nine others elsewhere.

You may need a little help, such as learning how to handle a microphone, how to time yourself, how to use your arms and facial gestures to back up the talk. But as you will see when I discuss professional ideas for platforms, there is very little difference between home speaking and downtown speaking.

My success in Baltimore showing merchants how to step

up sales, and in talking to their salespeople, I attracted the attention of the Hecht Company in Washington. I accepted a job for one year, full time, to show them how to put "Tested Selling Sentences" to use in their large store. They built me a most impressive "Word Laboratory," with all the fixtures from charts on the wall to black and white squared linoleum.

I have said several times the best thing to talk about is your own experiences, since they contain your own individual built-in enthusiasm; so I kept records and more records of my work at the Hecht Company.

Each department would tell me its present sales of an item it wanted to "push." I'd interview the salespeople on the item, then go behind the counter and test each bit of sales talk until I had arrived at the "Magic Words." Then I would take the salesgirls and salesmen and show them what to say and how to say it to make more sales. Then I would record the gains.

After one year, I had an accumulation of "before" and "after" records. Then I decided I had enough "experience" to go to New York City once more and try again to whip the Big Town.

HOW TO GREET PEOPLE YOU MEET

Make the other fellow happy—happy to have met you.

Don't make him twice glad, glad to have met you—glad he is leaving you.

Avoid such hackneyed greetings as, "How are you?" "Please ta meecha!" or the disinterested "Hello."

Also avoid such robust greetings as, "Put it there . . . !" You don't have to bowl over a fellow with your greeting, nor do you need to be trite or bland.

Try to say something that will interest him, or raise his ego, such as, "Bill has often spoken of you," or, "I have often wanted to meet you."

There are many little personal greetings that will immediately sell you to others such as: "Didn't I see you at the Jaycee dance?" "Are you related to Mayor Green?"

Personalize as much as possible, and when you are not able to, then use such complimentary words as: "It is a real pleasure to meet you." "I am very happy to meet Helen's friends."

People form snap judgments of your greeting. So make this first impression a favorable one for you.

5

Say Something Simple

When my year was up at the Hecht Company, I went to Macy's with my new firm title, the imposing "Tested Selling Institute and Word Laboratory." Macy's accepted me for a talk and I found myself once more on the august platform of the great Macy store, only this time without a single chart or graph.

I had learned one thing about charts and graphs, and I pass this on to you now: avoid them! Never hold them up in front of more than twenty-five people—because those in the rear can't see them. It is all right, on certain occasions, to read what may be in a chart or a graph or in a letter, providing you read it quickly and make it short.

The mind remembers only 15 per cent of what it hears, 85 per cent of what it sees, but if it can't see the graph then it is useless. Your listeners won't remember more than 15 per cent of what you describe to them.

It is also pointless to quote a long series of figures, wherein you try to show how many millions of customers bought something this year versus so many millions last year. These gigantic figures go in one ear and out the other.

It is perfectly all right, I found, to say, "This year the stocking industry sold 40 per cent more stockings than last year." People can remember the 40 per cent.

There are new machines on the market that can take a letter and blow it up to a size visible to more than twenty-five, but again the back row may fail to read more than a few billboard-type sentences. But investigate these new methods.

In a small group you can pass the charts and letters around. At a big meeting, tell those who are interested to come up after the talk and read them.

Unless you are in a statistical field, avoid charts and stand on your talk alone. Which is why I opened up at Macy's with my pet phrase: "I'd like to give you my personal experiences in Baltimore and at the Hecht Company of Washington that stepped up sales!"

My "personal experiences" included what we said, for example, to sell a chair in the furniture department. We told the women, "It is our favorite napping chair for husbands," and we sold out the chair. The chair buyer at Macy's sat up and took notice. He forgot how I looked, how I talked. He forgot my delivery. He whipped out a pad and pencil and wrote down my "magic phrase."

When I told about selling square fly swatters that were

fifteen cents against round ones at ten cents, the drug buyer marked down the sentence, "These are square, madam, and get them in the corners."

I was talking about things I knew, and that I knew would interest these people in New York. I was talking their own language, too.

New York, I found, was no different from Baltimore or Washington. Just larger. When I was called at Bloomingdale's, then Stern Brothers, then the Lerner Shops, J. C. Penney, Pennsylvania Drug Stores and others, I found people there who had "come from the sticks" themselves and were interested in "what makes people buy."

I learned that if a person buys a square clothespin in Baltimore because "it won't roll out of reach under a sink," people in any other city will buy the same idea. I learned that buyers buy ideas—not products. They buy what they feel the customer will buy.

On the whole, people everywhere will react to the same appeals of saving money, having less work to do, and receiving more fun, pleasure, health, happiness. These will interest the man in Hoboken just as much as the man in San Diego.

"That's a primate," says the teacher to the group of little girls around him. One girl asks, "What is a primate?" and he replies, "That's a monkey."

"Then why not say it is a monkey?" asks the little girl, with all the simplicity of a child.

Don't try to be brilliant in front of the patio group—or

26

the downtown Jaycee luncheon. You aren't selling your educational background, or your brilliance on a certain subject.

No one expects more than an ordinary speech from an ordinary guy. A helpful rule is this: *Say something simple!*

Another thing to remember is not to be a name-dropper. Don't feel you must say, "When General So-and-so and I were out fishing last week, the General said to me, 'Elmer, you are a great guy.' "

Who cares?

The group got together to learn how to make more money, gain greater happiness, get a new idea in living, or acquire better health from your experiences. Tell your story simply. Don't drag in well-known names simply for effect.

One great error to avoid is "talking down" to an audience you feel isn't as experienced as you are. You figure they are just youngsters, and so you try to talk in language you normally would never use.

It is curious that if a person wears a hearing aid we feel he isn't as alert as we are, and we try to spell out our meaning. Or if he speaks with an accent that he is an "uneducated foreigner."

On the other hand, it is often an error to try to use the technical language you feel is appropriate when you speak before a group of technicians. Just because you are explaining a new bookkeeping system to a group of engineers, there is no reason why you must assume the technical language of the engineer and sound ridiculous.

I found that department stores have a jargon, and when I could pick up a few of their trade words, that was okay, but I was not supposed to be an expert buyer—just a sales trainer—and there was no need for me to try to impress buyers by using trade words that came out of my mouth with a wobbly sound.

Talk their language, yes, where you can—but don't imagine a dentist wants you to show him how brilliant you are by using words taught him in medical school. He wants to learn one thing: how what you say will help him.

Tell him of your own experiences in terms you understand best. Use your own trade jargon providing he will comprehend it, and then invite him to "see how my own experiences may fit your field."

If you want to attract attention to your neckwear, make it loud. If you want to attract attention to your ideas, soften the neckwear.

If you want the other person to hear what you have to say, then say it in simple words. Don't flaunt your education before an audience of one or one hundred.

Learn Rule No. 4 in this chapter—*Say something simple* —and make sure what you say will interest the other person.

6

Throw Away the First Three Pages

As I sat recently at the head table of the New York Sales Executives Club and was told by Secretary Harry White that this was my fifteenth appearance there, I realized that this was where I got my first chance at a real public appearance.

It all happened one day when Kenneth Goode (creator of Little Johnny on the Philip Morris programs) needed a fill-in speaker and heard of my work with "Tested Selling Sentences."

"Come on over and tell our club members about your experiences in this interesting field of selling," he invited. He didn't say he had lost a speaker and that I was a substitute. I would have gone anyway for the chance to speak before this important group of top executives in the sales field.

I wrote out my speech. I took it to Ken Goode. He glanced through it quickly, then took the first three pages, tore them up, and threw them into a wastebasket and then said: "Start your speech here! Right in the middle!"

That was perhaps the greatest lesson I learned in writing out a speech. To write it out entirely—then throw away the first three pages!

That is what I did. I kept reading and rereading the remaining pages. I remembered all I could. I had been warned not to read the speech, but to write it out if I wanted to— then remember all I could, stand up and give it. What I failed to remember to tell them they wouldn't miss anyway.

I think this is fine advice for anyone. If you must write out a speech to help you co-ordinate your thinking, or to have a copy for the press, that is fine. But don't read it.

Use notes if you wish—but leave the written speech at home so you won't scare the audience when you walk to the podium armed with a thick manuscript!

Often when an audience sees this sheaf of papers under the arm of a speaker, they will sneak out the side doors before you are even introduced.

It is advisable to keep a record of all talks so that when you are invited back you won't repeat yourself. I now keep a record of each talk I make. Then when I am invited back a year or two later, I know which of my stories were told, and seldom do I repeat myself except in my formula for selling.

My formula is the five Wheelerpoints. They are the basis

of all my talks, and I learned after nineteen years of selling this single formula (with new examples) that it has become ingrained in American business.

A great error in speaking is to have too many points, rules or steps for the audience to remember. I have five. Dick Borden always had six. Zenn Kaufman has some ten short points.

As a newspaper reporter I learned that the more I wrote, the better I got. I was beginning to learn that the more I spoke, the quicker I got over my fear of people and of standing up before audiences.

Incidentally, I just read that Doris Day, the movie star, once "feared an audience even in her front room." That to perform in her own living room before friends "frightened her to death." She didn't appear frightened in that last movie I saw her in, so I guess others have overcome their anxieties in meeting people and talking in front of them.

As a reporter I practiced writing. I'd even invent stunts such as hiking around the country to see if bums really got apple pie handouts. As an amateur speaker, I now went out of the way in New York to get speaking engagements. I landed the Kiwanis, Rotary and Lions clubs my first year, and had plenty of proving grounds to stretch out my speaking legs.

The more speaking I did, the more fluent I became. I always had a curb conference with myself immediately after each talk, wherein I would weigh my audience reaction and try to overcome any weaknesses.

I would make mental notes of points that went over, and I'd keep them in my speeches. I'd make notes of the parts of my talk that failed, and I'd try to strengthen them or leave them out. I practiced proper spacing of my ideas. I practiced proper speed of delivery so I didn't talk too fast —the big mistake of beginners so scared they want to get it over with—or so slow that I bored my audience.

Perhaps the greatest thing I learned in these early days was the tip-off given me by Ken Goode.

I'll give it to you once more, so you'll remember it: *Throw away the first three pages. No one will ever miss them!*

7

Six Simple Steps to Conquer Fear of Meeting People

Knowing you are good makes you good. To be a poised speaker, you need to build up your confidence to a point where fear leaves you. Confidence comes from experience and the knowledge that you have something to say that people want to hear.

Here is how I perked up my confidence. I started in Baltimore by talking to a few clerks on selling. My talk went over for the audience was small. My ego rose.

Then I went to larger stores. My confidence rose again. Then I had my own single store, the Hecht Company, where I spoke and met people and increased sales.

Later I spoke at Macy's, at Bloomingdale's, and at Stern

Brothers. My confidence continued to grow because I had an important message to tell, and I had learned how to tell it.

One day a man sent a card into my new office at the Hotel Pennsylvania (later the Hotel Statler) in New York. (I had a deal with the hotel to help them sell higher-priced rooms in exchange for one for an office for myself.) The card said, H. W. HOOVER, PRESIDENT, THE HOOVER COMPANY. This struck me as an unfunny practical joke. I kept him waiting ten minutes. You know, once he came in it took me another twenty minutes to realize this really was the president of the famous vacuum cleaner company. He had read about my work in *Reader's Digest*.

"What can you do for us?" was his question, simply stated. "Let me tell you my experiences with cleaners in Baltimore," I replied.

I represented Mr. Hoover and his firm for twelve years.

Don't bluff your way. I could have put on a big front with Mr. Hoover and the others, but somehow I had just too much of the small town in me to want to, and I certainly didn't look the part to get away with a bluff either. I still looked like Joe College.

All I had was one phrase, "Let me tell you my experiences with what you are making and selling."

That magic phrase kept me alive, for people pay money for practical experiences.

Then came invitations to speak before the sales meetings

34

of these firms. It was fortunate I had the Baltimore experience, then the New York retail experience to build my confidence before talking to groups of hard-boiled manufacturers' salesmen.

Don't tell experts how to do their jobs. In speaking to experts, admit that you do not know their business, but that you have had some experience along similar lines and hope they can use it.

Experience selling a vacuum cleaner can be used in selling insurance, and experience in selling underwear at Macy's can be used to show the Hathaway Shirt folks how to merchandise their product.

Tell your story simply and directly. Skip the technical language. Emphasize the points that can be used by the experts in your audience, but don't try to teach them their business.

No one likes to be preached to. So keep your talk friendly and modest. Avoid any statements or mannerisms that might brand you as a "know-it-all." Pedantry is for people who use knowledge as an excuse to flaunt themselves, strut their stuff, impress with words of wisdom.

The greatest of platform speakers sound simple. So simple you forget them and hear their ideas. Once you "hear" the speaker, you are through with that speaker. You hear him, and not his ideas. Let them hear your ideas and not you.

People come to your home to hear you tell them things

that will entertain them, inform them, or make them happy with you. They come to a sales meeting or downtown luncheon meeting to hear the very same things.

They don't come to "hear" you, but to hear what you have to say!

So have something to say. Otherwise keep quiet. You can't learn when your mouth is open, but when it does open make sure the other person will learn something, enjoy something, be happier for having listened to you.

Stand up, say something, sit down! That's a mighty good rule to practice in overcoming fear of people, in gaining courage to meet strangers, friends, the neighbor next door.

Unless you are an expert on funny stories, a Milton Berle or Bob Hope, then leave the stories to the TV stars. Be content to give a "few words" on the topic in which you excel. There is a time and place to tell the funny story. There is an entire chapter coming up on this, but until you are a master of stories, let the experts tell them. Be content to tell how you grew the best or worst petunias in town, how you developed a new idea, or how you process orders in your company.

Conquering fear of people boils itself down to knowing what to say and how to say it, so that when you stand up and face that cold room of people, you can close your eyes, if you want, and start reciting your experiences.

8

How to Overcome Stage Fright

Stage fright is a horrible thing. Some people cannot walk into a room filled with friends without uneasiness and discomfort.

In our own public-speaking courses we instruct our group directors, on the first night, to have the class merely stand up, give their names and occupations, and then sit down. Some almost choke on saying their names.

I can remember my own stage fright at meeting the famous George Washington Hill, Jr., the Lucky Strike king, in his own kingdom. For two days I trembled at the thought of meeting the famous man, known for his fetish of wearing a hat at a conference table and for throwing a glass of water across the table to prove some point.

The day arrived. I took two members of my three-member staff (including the secretary) and invaded the lair of the lion. There he sat as I had visualized, down at the end of the table nervously tapping his fingers for I was two minutes late.

"What's this 'Tested Selling Sentences' all about?" he snapped, and sixteen of his staff members came to attention. All riveted their eyes on me.

I tried to speak. I failed. I was tongue-tied. The lion had me treed. My courage failed me. I stammered and stuttered something. I don't know what it was to this day. The lion looked at me as a lion would look at a mouse, wondering what in thunder the mouse was up to. He had expected a derby-and-cane presentation of my case, and he was prepared for that sort of interview.

Instead, he saw a scared youth trying to talk to him. More or less in amusement at having been inveigled into the situation, I guess, he said: "Tell me about your experiences using words to make people buy."

He had actually given me my opening phrase. He wanted to hear my experiences. My tongue-tied words straightened out. I had been given a reprieve. At once I started off with, "My experiences in using the right words to make people buy go back to the time I was selling space in newspapers. It was back in Baltimore . . ." As I talked Mr. Hill relaxed, sat back, and when I had finished all he said was: "How much will a job cost Lucky Strike?"

Again I was floored. I knew if I was too low, I'd sound cheap. If I was too high, he'd probably toss me out the door. Should I have the courage to say a hundred thousand

38

dollars—fifty thousand—twenty-five thousand? I gulped out, "Five thousand dollars."

"You mean a week?" he said, raising his eyebrows. I stammered, "No—a month."

"Is that as cheap as you'll work?" he asked. I said, "Yes," my knees shaking, for my price up to that time had been about a thousand dollars for the entire service.

If I had lacked the courage to say five thousand dollars a month, I'd have been doing the job very much underpaid. As it was, I had a good income for many months, that allowed me a chance to do a nation-wide sales service for this big cigarette firm.

One day the head of the Texas Company came to me. H. W. Dodge in person. I told him of my Baltimore experiences in selling gasoline and oils and related items. This time I figured the job was worth ten thousand dollars.

I had learned now the art of speaking with others, not fearing even presidents of firms, so when this sales head asked me the price, I said, "Ten thousand dollars for a thorough job." I hadn't realized how weak my voice must have been. How scared I must have looked when I let those big words "ten thousand dollars" out of my mouth. I had never quoted that much money before in all my life.

I failed by letting my voice drop. I made the cardinal error of quoting a price, then stopping my presentation, thus allowing the price to sink in.

The deeper it sank in, the more my face must have given me away. Mr. Dodge evidently felt a little sorry for me.

He came around beside me and sat in a chair. He put his hand on my arm and said, "Elmer, can't you do it for five thousand?"

I did.

I had learned a great lesson in overcoming fear of others. Go around and sit side by side with them. Get close to them. This lesson cost me five thousand dollars. I hope reading of it here will save you money.

On the platform, don't try to reach out to an audience scattered in the rear of the room. If they fail to sit close to you, then get the chairman to ask them to move up to the front rows.

In smaller groups, walk around the imposing speaker's table, and stand in the midst of them. You will be closer to them physically—and mentally.

Stage fright often results when people are too far away from you. Note how in your living room, den or porch, you find people sliding chairs closer to each other. Few people have fear when huddled close to each other.

At small sales meetings, I learned to walk away from the podium and "be one of the gang." The gang liked my friendliness, and their nearness gave me strength in added courage.

This is an important lesson in gaining courage. Put it to daily use. Never let anything get between you and the other person.

The closer you are to people, the less fear you'll have, and the more courage you'll gain.

40

HOW TO SHAKE HANDS TO WIN FRIENDS

Your handshake should express your confidence, sincerity and friendliness. It is often a first impression on others. Therefore make it "sell" you.

THE WHEELER WAY

Use the Elmer Wheeler Handshake by gripping the hand firmly, comfortably.

Put your right foot slightly forward to give you balance. It makes the other person feel you are BENDING toward his FRIENDSHIP.

The shake is simple: just two short UPS AND DOWNS as you greet the other person. ONE UP and DOWN indicates disinterest. THREE seems overdoing it.

This Tested Handshake is a real Friend-Maker!

HANDSHAKING "DON'TS"

    The Ring Squeezer
    The Fish Hand
    The Bone Crusher
    The Hand Pumper
    The Hand Jerker
    The Glue Hand

AVOID these handshakes. They make bad "first impressions"; they lose friends.

9

When You Find Yourself
in Hot Water

The phrase "Don't Sell the Steak—Sell the Sizzle" gave me a trade-mark in the industry, and on the platform. Trade-marks are important to any speaker or business person.

Now I don't mean you must wear a Frank Buck hat, or smoke a big cigar like Groucho to get trade-marked, but if there is something that will identify you, in a dignified manner, you will be remembered more readily.

If you plan to make a reputation as a speaker, you might start thinking about your trade-mark, as I did. I hit upon the sizzle (and a bow tie) because it told such a big story about what makes people buy. In one sentence "sizzle" brought up a tremendous, thought-provoking idea.

When you said, "Oh, he's the man with the red suspenders," everybody knew you were talking about our old friend Sam Vining, who so identified himself for years with his audiences.

"He's the man who throws the sledgehammer at his audience" always identifies Zenn Kaufman and his balsam-wood hammer.

Others are identified by mannerisms, methods of dress, style of delivery.

Knowing you have an identification helps overcome fear of going over with an audience, and slowing down, relaxing before a talk or a meeting with people, helps overcome worry about meeting them.

You can banish worry by first banishing haste.

Rushing onto a platform, into a meeting room or the den of a friend, all out of breath, in great haste to do nothing more than arrive, upsets your tempo, increases your blood pressure and makes you stammer and stutter.

A breathless person gives a weak speech.

Then he begins to worry, "Am I going over?" Worry kills the rest of the speech. A reasonable amount of worry is fine. It shows you want to be a perfectionist. But don't over-worry.

Should you memorize a speech?

Perhaps the greatest worry of all is, "Should you memorize your speech?" Possibly more people ask me that question than any other, and the answer is very simple: Become as familiar as possible with your speech beforehand, then forget your worries and give it. People will never miss what they never hear.

Sure, you will forget it in parts; but your enthusiasm will carry you over. If you worry about remembering points, then jot a few points down—but don't ever, ever read a speech. If your speech is mimeographed, pass it around. Don't bother to read it. People can take it home and read it at their leisure, and you can sit down and relax.

Among the hazards of public speaking is the unexpected complication. Let me give you three examples of how I, through no fault of my own, found myself in hot water.

I had been invited to Montreal to speak at the Sales Executives Club there, and I had no more than gotten my speech under way with the slogan, "Don't Sell the Steak— Sell the Sizzle" when someone in the back row hollered, "Baloney."

This, you will agree, was somewhat disconcerting. I had learned, though, "never to fight city hall—or an audience," so I merely smiled and went on selling my sizzle.

Once again the voice yelled, "Baloney," and this time I stopped talking and asked whether the fellow wanted to step up and sell his baloney to us all. Sure enough, he did. He came up to the platform. I invited him to sit down on the platform. He did. The audience was wondering how this little scene would turn out.

"Up here it's real baloney," next announced the self-appointed critic of Elmer Wheeler. I asked whether he would like to speak his piece over the microphone for five minutes, after which I'd take over. I hoped the club heads would catch on to my difficulty, and come to my rescue.

Believe it or not, the chap did stand up at the microphone and start to recite Shakespeare. The last we saw of him he was between two policemen being carried to the door.

Later, I again found myself in hot water. This time, I spoke a month after Dale Carnegie on the platform of the famous Massey Hall in Toronto, with three thousand people in the audience.

There I was in the midst of my speech on "Selling the Sizzle," when my fingers struck some chewing gum on the podium. As my hand raised toward the ceiling, so did the gum. There I stood, frozen, with gum a yard long between me and the elegant podium. The polite Canadian audience looked on in amazement. They were too good an audience to giggle; but seeing me in hot water, they wondered what I'd do.

I knew I didn't dare overlook the gum. It would take me five minutes to get it all wiped off. What could I do to turn this unfortunate accident to my advantage? An idea hit me. I looked at my hand, the gum, and then the audience, and said: "Has Dale Carnegie been here lately?"

That's all it took. The house came down. I had five minutes of noisy laughter during which to get rid of my gum.

At the Abilene, Texas, High School one night, I had no more than gotten warmed up before the audience of salespeople and business executives, when someone tossed a home-made bomb into the room.

It was hand-made—but it had a fuse and the fuse was going.

Luckily someone was close enough to pick up the bomb and toss it out the window. I knew exactly what would happen. It came flying back in through another window. This time near me. I took one look at the fuse, saw I had a chance, and tossed it out again. This time it went off. With not much of a boom, but loud enough.

A few minutes later three young boys were caught back-stage for the act, and when the law asked me what I'd like done, I said, "Make 'em sit on the platform and listen to the rest of my speech!"

I have often worried about drunks in an audience. How can you handle them?

When a drunk got too noisy at the St. Louis Realtors banquet several years ago in the Hotel Jefferson, I learned a trick: Lower the voice—and highlight the noise.

When people get noisy, lower your voice. Others around the noise can't hear you and they, not you, will shush up the noisemaker. Try this when you are worried about a boisterous audience.

Again, you will find yourself in still hotter water if, when someone straggles in late, you glare at him, address remarks to him, or otherwise let the audience know you disapprove of his late arrival.

Try turning your head to another part of the auditorium, so the latecomer won't annoy you. But never say anything to him.

Another good rule to keep worry off the platform is: Never talk politics; never discuss religion.

I am assuming these are not your speech subjects. If they are, then that is fine; but to bring in politics and religion needlessly merely leads to loss of part of your audience.

So to win friends when speaking, avoid controversial subjects. Let the experts deal in these subjects—subjects that can bring worry to nonspecialists.

Learn to relax your worries away. Sit quietly before the speech. Be content with the knowledge that you know more than the audience about your subject, and that they want to hear your experiences.

Smile when you reach the platform. Smile sincerely. This will win over the audience in a hurry. Most audiences expect a speaker to be poker-faced. Fool them—smile.

Don't walk on with a sheaf of papers. You'll scare the life out of the audience, who'll assume they have to sit through an hour of long-winded reading.

If, as may happen, you find yourself confronted with an unforeseen interruption, keep your head. Usually, you'll manage to find a way to turn the unpleasantness to your advantage.

10

How to Remember Names

Almost everyone will tell you, "I can remember faces but I can't remember names."

They forgot they were not born with a bad memory. A bad memory is always cultivated.

I have lost many friends because I failed to remember names. Yet to remember names isn't difficult, and it will help banish fear of meeting strangers. Some people can't even remember the names of the first two people they are introduced to. Why? Mainly because they don't want to remember them.

There are three simple rules for remembering names. Rule one is: Hear the name.

Most people fail to hear the name in the first place, and if you don't hear a name how can you possibly remember it? It is no error in etiquette to say, "I didn't hear your name." The other person is actually flattered that you want to hear it, and he will repeat it.

This time focus attention on the name. Make sure you hear it—and hear it correctly. Then put the next rule to use. That is: Repeat the name. By repeating it you impress it upon your memory, so find excuses to repeat a name you wish to remember. Say, "What is your opinion, Mrs. Henrietti, of this new book?" or, "I think you are right, Mrs. Henrietti." Use her name over and over. If she leaves you after a hurried introduction, then say it to yourself over and over.

When you have met several people, repeat the few names you have heard, and try to identify them with something about their faces, dress or mannerisms.

Then come back and hear a few more names. Until you are an expert, don't try to meet everybody all at once. Meet them in groups.

Then try the third rule: Associate the name.

By associating the name you have a double chance to recall it at will, especially if the association is ridiculous, humorous or dramatic. For example, say to yourself: "Mrs. Henrietti—a ready hen." Or, "Mr. Pigg—a hog—pig, hog."

If you can go up to someone and use his name, you will feel a new confidence. This will make you forget your stage fright, your fear of being with strangers.

As my new-found work, that of sales training and public speaking, grew by leaps and bounds, I found that one of my greatest assets was remembering names and faces. For people like to hear their names.

Writing names in a book, with an identification word or two beside each, will help you. One trick of the trade I found interesting was invented by a service station attendant.

I often wondered how he remembered my name, until one day I saw he had it written inside my gas tank cap.

Another service station advises all its workers to write, in chalk, the name of the car owner underneath the floor boards when the car is first greased. So the next time the car is serviced, the attendant can use the man's name as though he remembered it.

Here are the three rules to remember names: Hear the name. Repeat the name. Associate the name.

Another important point is to speak clearly.

As I look back to the time when I hated to meet strangers, stand up and speak to people, I feel that my greatest handicap was failure in properly enunciating my words.

Fail to use your voice—and it will fail you when you try. I found this true as I began to talk before the salespeople in Baltimore. I lacked proper voice enunciation.

Later in this book I will tell you how it once took me two hours to say, "He's a DuMont dealer," for a movie, but if I had had the "Please pass the potatoes, Percy" training this might not have happened.

Certain tones of voice can break glasses clear across a room, as General Electric has proved time and time again by sending out sound waves on tuning forks.

It is said that the walls of Jericho tumbled because the

sound of the trumpets was synchronized with the mortar
and caused it to crumble; and I know Caruso could smash
a glass or crack a mirror when his voice hit certain tones.

On the boat ride from Seattle to Alaska, a big stunt is for
the captain to blow the boat's horn and start an avalanche of
ice from the high banks down to the water's edge. I know the
proper tone of voice can make or break any one of us.

So in our Elmer Wheeler Institute we have tried many
stunts to help people enunciate properly. One of the best
is our Percy stunt.

In this you face a lighted candle about fifteen inches from
your mouth and say, "Please pass the potatoes, Percy," and
if you have good enunciation, the candle will be snipped out
by the sound waves.

Not by the loudness of the voice, but by the *tone* of the
sound waves.

In fact, you can yell at the candle and nothing will happen. Try it. But if you have good enunciation it will set up
sound waves that will bend the light of the candle clear
over, and finally put it out.

Now this isn't as easy as it sounds. You will be inclined
to blow your breath on the candle instead of letting your
sound waves do the work.

You will also be inclined to yell at the candle, and otherwise set up a big disturbance, when the simplest statement
of "Please pass the potatoes, Percy" in the right tone of voice
will zing out the light.

51

I can only say in passing that this is another proof that in life it isn't so much what you do as how you do it that counts.

If you will fix this one thought firmly in your mind, you will do much toward eliminating fear, anxiety and worry over meeting strangers; toward overcoming stage fright in standing up before clients, friends or the downtown club—or before a jury if you are an attorney.

Practice making your words come out properly so that even the back row can hear the softest whisper. Shouting will fail, whereas the low voice of a firm speaker will be far more impressive.

Let "Please pass the potatoes, Percy" help you overcome and banish your fears of talking with people—or to people.

11

36 Dos and Don'ts Plus 8 Common Errors

I am finding as the years go by, and platforms come and go, that speaking to others is salesmanship! That selling ideas to groups is not different from selling ideas (or products) to individuals.

Many of the rules used by salesmen to make sales can be used by the speaker to sell audiences.

I have jotted down many "dos" and "don'ts" for speakers, that I have collected over nineteen years, which will help any person, whether he is talking to a neighbor over a back fence or to a Board of Directors at a bank. Here they are:

1. Start each talk with a punch sentence that gets immediate attention.
2. Tell the audience why you are there.
3. Make a point—then go on to another.

4. Never read a speech.

5. Don't have a dozen anticlimaxes.

6. Make jokes fit your speech.

7. Don't talk in a monotone.

8. Stand still while speaking.

9. Don't have distracting mannerisms.

10. Be brief.

11. Work to a climax, then sit down.

12. Make good use of facial gestures.

13. Synchronize arm movements with thoughts.

14. Use simple words.

15. Sell your ideas—not your education.

16. Let the introducer do the bragging about you.

17. Don't preach.

18. Don't point fingers at the audience.

19. Stay away from the water jug.

20. Don't slouch over a mike.

21. Forget the mike. It won't bite you.

22. Use many "for examples."

23. Use question marks, not crowbars.

24. Forget Pat and his friend Mike.

25. Say something simple.

26. Practice . . . practice . . . practice.

27. Use your mirror.

28. Keep your eye on the audience.

29. Always summarize your points.

30. Ask for action at the end.

31. Don't be pedantic.
32. Don't talk DOWN to the audience.
33. Don't speak too slowly—or too rapidly.
34. Be honest.
35. Be sincere.
36. Be confident.

Put these thirty-six pointers to effective use. They aren't designed only for public speakers and national lecturers, but for anyone who must speak to others in public, if only to say, "Hello, how are you today?"

Let me give you now what my experience has taught me are the greatest errors made by speakers.

1. Some people talk too much. They won't pause long enough for the other person to grasp what is being said.

2. People say "I" too much. A reporter prefers to say "we" and "our." But "I" is the smallest word in the world—"you" is the biggest.

3. People talk too long. They get worked up over their story, and fail to bring it to an end. Long-winded speakers, on street corners, in homes, on platforms, are bores.

4. People fail to make a good start with their speech. They also fail to have an ending that summarizes their speech and asks the audience to do something about the talk. Never let an audience walk away saying, "What was he driving at?"

5. People rant and rave on platforms. They feel they must yell and scream like movie politicians, otherwise they won't go over. Emphasize your talk on and off—but not all of the time.

6. People underestimate the intelligence of others. They have been taught the average person has the intelligence of a twelve-year-old. So watch out that you don't talk DOWN to your group.

7. People never know when to shut up. They tell and retell the same thing over and over, like a phonograph record that is cracked. Speak your piece, stop talking, sit down.

8. People read their speeches, refer too often to charts and graphs, keep putting on and taking off their glasses to read. This is very annoying to an audience. Memorize the main points you want to get over, and have them written in big type on a card or two.

There are other errors that are common to beginners in speaking, or in trying to win over friends, employers, employees, but in the main, if you will avoid making these eight errors, you will find your talk going over and your fear flying out the door.

5 TESTED FRIEND-MAKERS

1. *"I am proud of you!"* The five best words to make people feel good. Try them on the boss, employee, wife, husband, friend. You elevate their ego—and they'll never let you down.

2. *"What is YOUR opinion?"* The four greatest words to gain willing information from the toughest person or utter stranger. You compliment their judgment. They like that.

3. *"If you please!"* Three magic words to get fast action out of people for the things and favors you ask of them. Tag this on to all requests.

4. *"Thank you!"* Two words to make people GLAD they did a favor. Never fail to use them. "Thank you" is in every language.

5. *"YOU! !"* The one word to make the most friends. People like to hear about THEMSELVES. So use YOU—never "I," the smallest word in the world.

> Keep these friend-makers in your DAILY possession. They will be a constant reminder of how to SELL YOURSELF to others.

12

How to Tell Stories

Pat and Mike passed out with vaudeville. But the joy of telling a funny story still remains.

I have promised, as we go along, that I'd pass on experiences of the pros for your use.

So let me tell you what experience will bear out on the art and science of telling a funny story and having people laugh at it—not at you.

Tell your stories Jack Benny style.

This is the technique of making fun of yourself, not of others. It is the knack of telling humorous incidents on yourself, wherein you are the butt of the joke, not the other fellow.

Never personalize a story by using the names of people in the room or in the audience. Sure, they laugh. You have forced them to laugh at the joke so they will not be thought poor sports. Inside, however, they resent your making them the butt of your joke.

We have a session in our training schools wherein each student in turn must stand up and tell a humorous story to start off his speech.

He is warned in advance that the story must be one that naturally and normally weaves into his speech, highlights a point or otherwise fits the occasion. Merely to drag in a current story that proves nothing nor fits anything you are about to say is bad practice.

A pointless story is as bad as a pointless joke. It may be harmless, but it gets you nowhere, and only too often everybody has heard it and they nudge each other knowingly.

It is said that a Britisher laughs at a joke the next day, the Russian never laughs at it; and the American nudges a friend and says, "I heard that one before." Jokes, therefore, are dangerous. Unless they are woven into your speech.

Ending a speech with a funny story is risky, for if too many have heard it the last thing you leave with the audience is that knowing nudge and the murmur around the room, "I heard that one before."

When you do end with a funny story, make it prove the point of your talk. Don't drag in the latest funny yarn unless it backs up your talk.

Don't gamble on losing the importance of your talk with a story that may flop.

This technique of "fitting the joke to the talk," used by the professionals, applies to any part of the talk. There is no excuse for telling a joke unless it carries your thoughts one step closer to the goal you had in mind in giving the talk.

Funny stories, in the hands of experts, sell an idea for a speaker faster than anything else. A funny story, properly placed, can defeat an opponent in a courtroom debate or in a race for political office.

It is not good taste to be too much of a wisecracker with bon mots that bring smiles but that also bring envy and resentment.

People don't like clever speakers. Being a smart aleck on the platform, with wisecracks and pert remarks, humorous as they may be, won't win you friends or votes.

People buy your sincerity first.

You may split infinitives and forget to pause, or talk too fast or too slowly, but the audience will excuse all this if you sound sincere and are sincere.

Wisecrack—and you'll lose them, no matter how Princetonian a polish you have on the platform.

People buy sincerity on the platform, not acquired polish.

Emily Post teaches us which fork to use at which course. It is just as important to know which story to tell at which gathering.

The Pullman story is okay, perhaps, with a small group of cronies, but you gamble with it among strangers. Certainly it won't go over with the Wednesday Afternoon Ladies' Society.

Learn never to tell stories that ridicule religious groups

60

or cliques. Let the Irish tell stories on the Irish, the Jews on themselves, but don't you try to tell an Irish or Jewish story unless you are noted for them and are an expert.

Learn that off-color stories are no good these days, even before a hard-boiled group of salesmen. Too many sales managers feel that the yarn about the farmer's daughter is what puts them over with their men. This is not true.

I recall the yarn about the speaker who said, "Since this is an all-stag audience, with no ladies present, I imagine I can tell a few farmer stories," to which a dignified man in the back row got up and said, "There may not be ladies present, sir, but there are gentlemen."

Somebody must listen when a story is told, and until I could tell them myself, I was the world's best audience—and I won friends, and accounts, by being on hand with a ready laugh at some purchasing agent's humorous story.

I learned one trick in laughing. Never overdo it. Don't put too much into the laugh, or the clever teller will soon sense you are leading him on, perhaps for a job, an account or an order.

Laugh easily, with no guffaws. Often a smile tells the other person you appreciated his yarn. No need to slap him on the back and shout, "Boy, can *you* tell funny stories!"

Don't egg on a storyteller. Ask him once or twice to tell a story you like, but don't embarrass him by pressing him.

When he tells a funny story, don't break into the laughter with, "That reminds *me* of one." Let the laugh have its full attention, then bring up your own story. Don't kill the other person's story by driving one of yours right on top of it.

One other tip: *Don't tell long-winded stories!*

It may be a good one, but if it is too long, it will surely bore others, especially those burning with a "quickie" to tell themselves.

If it is one of those classics you hear, and you are a real storyteller, maybe you can get away with the long story in a small group.

On the platform, though, you can't get away with it. The average platform talk at noon is about twenty-five minutes, at night around forty-five minutes. So don't be a story hog!

If you are called upon to say a "few words," and all you have is a story, fine—if it proves a point. But tell it, then sit down.

Never try to explain a story. If it needs explanation, you need another story.

Tell your story, sit down, relax, let someone else have his go at storytelling. Avoid laughing too much at your own story, else you'll spoil it for others. Often a little laughter on your part is provocative. It shows you are enjoying the telling of the story.

The big trick in telling interesting stories, of course, is to tell your own experiences. You just can't get away from this greatest of all rules in holding attention.

You will crowd around the storyteller as he takes you through the side streets of Paris, what he saw in the shows, what he experienced on top of the Eiffel Tower. You will thrill with him in Rome and Denmark and China, as he tells you his experiences and adventures. Provided, of course, he *is* interesting and not just long-winded.

People love to listen to the experiences of others. That is why they attend lectures of famous travelers. People relive their own experiences and daydream about their experiences to be, when you talk about yours.

But don't feel you must have a punch line each time you tell an experience or relate an adventure.

It is vital to every speaker to learn the simple ways to hold attention by good conversation, almost a lost art these days of movies and TV.

13

If You Dress Better You'll Speak Better

I don't believe a two-hundred-dollar suit makes the speech any better; but I do believe the right clothes will make you feel better.

I am often asked my thinking on what a person should wear when he or she talks at an average luncheon meeting, dinner or banquet. Can clothes really make the man?

People come to hear the speaker and not to "hear" the clothes he wears, unless of course the speaker is a designer, a famous personality or the owner of a clothing company. Then his clothing might be part of what people come to see.

I prefer letting them see me—not my haberdashery or suit.

The average person should dress down. He should find out first if evening wear is required. If so, then that is all there is to it. You go in the "uniform" of the typical chicken-and-apple-pie lecturer.

If it is a noon luncheon or a non-dress-up banquet, then dress simply. I'll tell you my experiences in learning about proper dress.

I found that if I wore a dark suit and a light shirt, perhaps white or off-white, then the light of my shirt against the dark of my suit highlighted my face. The eyes of the audience then rested on my facial expressions and not on my suit.

I have learned, too, to wear a bow necktie. This is my own preference based perhaps on the fact that it covers less of my shirt and so permits more of the white to reflect on my face where every speaker wants his audience to concentrate. The fact that bow ties accumulate less banquet soup may also have been a deciding factor in my choice of them.

I learned, too, from the apple-pie-and-chicken circuit that the pocket handkerchief should just peek out of my pocket, and not be flying in the breeze.

One day an observant philosopher said to me: "Elmer, did you ever notice the more egotistical a person, the more his handkerchief sticks out of his pocket?"

I became mighty conscious after that of just how far my handkerchief poked out of my pocket.

I learned, too, to keep my ties and socks dark in color. This keeps the eyes of the audience away from them. As to jewelry, I found one ring to be satisfactory, and not a large

65

one either, and that my watch was better on a leather band rather than an expensive-looking gold one that was distracting.

Indeed, I learned how to "hide" Elmer—and highlight his words.

I never realized until some two thousand speeches too late that the speech begins the moment the speaker walks onto the platform. While he is sitting by waiting to be introduced, he is under observation and must watch every move he makes.

This applies while he is sitting at the luncheon or dinner table. How he eats, how he handles his fork, how he smokes or converses, smiles or scowls, can make or break a man before he reaches the podium.

I have seen people watch me lap my soup, butter my bread, etc. For years I never bothered much, but when I suddenly realized the speech had begun the minute I entered the room, from that day on I watched my peas and manners.

I now watch how I walk into a room. How I shake hands, making sure to do it simply and easily—no wallops on the back, no pump handles, no ring squeezing.

I found that people can see your shoes as you stand by a podium, and if they are not shined or have worn heels, people form snap judgments of your speech and figure it too is worn at the heels.

It didn't take me long to learn that, especially before chamber meetings or those of merchants, each person saw something different when he looked up at me.

The tie man saw my tie. The shirt man my shirt. The clothing man my suit. The jeweler my jewelry. The shoe man my shoes and socks.

So I found it less expensive to buy expensive things. You can't deduct them from your income tax, but you will gain a lot of respect by having a "speaker's wardrobe" *just for the occasion* when you stand up in front of an audience.

You have no inventory as a speaker other than a good suitcase, one the airlines find it hard to bang up; plus a fine wardrobe of "speaking clothes." The carpenter buys the best of hammers and saws. It's his stock in trade. As one who appears before audiences, your stock in trade is the clothing you wear.

14

How I Learned Not to Buck a Trend

I was indeed riding high, wide and handsome that Sunday morning I remember so well, when the Japs hit Pearl Harbor.

Things had moved nicely for me in New York City. I had gone farther there than I had ever dreamed, with an office at 521 Fifth Avenue, a nice address for a fellow born on an ordinary street in life.

Accounts were coming to me at last. I was happily helping Cadillac sell more of their cars. And I was working on a prolonged tour of speaking for such firms as Western Union, Sears, Aetna Life and others.

Then came the war.

Almost every single account asked me to defer my contract "until we get something to sell again." Here I was, a sales expert with nothing to help people to sell. A speaker without a message.

The draft caught me about the first month of World War II. But I was determined not to be drafted, so I went to a sentry at Arlington in Virginia. He must have thought me crazy when I said, "Is this where a fellow can get a commission in the Marine Corps?"

He said it was. He telephoned some colonel and said, "There's a fellow here, sir, who wants a commission. Shall I send him up?" There was a long pause. A smile came to the sentry's face. He told me, "See Colonel So-and-so."

The Colonel was taken aback by the straightforward sentence, "I've got experience I think the Marines can use. I'd like a commission."

Without doubt hundreds of others had asked for commissions through congressmen, senators and governors, but here was a guy, hat in hand, saying he had experience the Marines might use.

"Let's take a walk," said the Colonel, after he had heard my experiences making people buy and in public speaking. He led me in and out of several offices, and finally a Colonel Wheeler was introduced to me.

The Colonel had a hobby of studying the origin of the name Wheeler. I spent two hours with him telling him of my family history and experiences, and when I left he said, "We can use a good speaker in officer procurement. You'll hear from me."

As a space salesman for the Hearst newspapers, and later for my own firm, now with the more subdued title of Tested Selling, Inc., I had learned one lesson—that a sale isn't a sale until you get the other fellow's signature.

I was promised a commission in the Marines. But the draft was too close for me to gamble, so I went over to an office in the Navy Department and used the same approach. I was sent from office to office by amused, but interested, officers until I hit the Public Relations Department.

I told my story. It so happened the man was looking for a chap like me to get up and talk Navy to service clubs. Just my meat, but alas, I was forty pounds overweight!

"I'll get it waived for you," said the Lieutenant Commander in charge. "We need good speakers like you."

So I went back to my new home in Dallas, Texas, where I had finally moved from New York City, although I kept the office in New York.

Time went on. Finally the week of my induction arrived, and I wired both the Marines and the Navy. I had only seven days left.

The Navy wired back to get into V-11, which was the "protective division" where the Navy placed a man they wanted for future use. On the morning of the seventh day I walked down to the post office and was sworn in.

Next morning, by special delivery, I got a big letter from the Marine Corps addressed to Captain Elmer Wheeler.

Imagine as a Navy Third Class Seaman suddenly getting

a commission as Captain in the Marine Corps. I ask you, what would you do?

I rushed back to the Navy and showed them my commission. One and all laughed at me as they said, "You're in the Navy now, sailor." I was finally told, with heavy sarcasm, by the Chief, "You can always call Commandant Rosenthal in New Orleans."

That is exactly what I did, and an emergency call, too, for wasn't my future an emergency?

I got the Commandant so fast it took my breath away and I told him the story of what had happened. I made it sound good. He, too, told me it was too late. That I was a Navy man now.

Then a lucky thought came to me. I said: "Sir, I have certain experiences the Marine Corps wants, which is why they rushed me the commission—and after all, sir, I'll still be Navy anyway, won't I?"

He paused. He laughed. He said, "You win. You'll still be Navy. I'll teletype your release."

Life in the Marine Corps was fine—but not for a public speaker. I spent time at Parris Island, New River, Quantico, and finally ended up in Officer Procurement in Kansas City.

I started speaking at service clubs, but this was my downfall. I was always billed as "Elmer the Sizzler," not as "Captain Wheeler of the Marine Corps." Finally the Marines called me back to Washington.

The colonel in charge said, "We'll make a deal with you,

Captain. You seem to have speaking ability, but people want to hear the experiences and adventures of Elmer the salesman, and not Captain Wheeler the Marine. In fact, as a forty-pound-overweight Marine, you haven't had any experiences yet, and besides you don't look like a Marine. So—"

I have been out on twenty-four-hours call ever since.

Firms and chambers of commerce and merchants associations, with a war boom on and no merchandise, wanted nothing to do with learning how to sell what they didn't have.

I was told to wait until the war was over. But that might be years. I was without a client, and needed money. My sales books were selling very poorly, and then one day a J. C. Penney man gave me a seventy-thousand-dollar idea.

He said, "Why not tell my clerks how to take an hour to say No instead of shouting to customers there's a war on?"

I liked the idea. I wrote an article called, "Elmer's Little Black Notebook," wherein I told about the salespeople, hotel clerks and waiters who were getting into my little black notebook "for their discourtesies, impoliteness and bad manners."

I gave the article away free to the National Junior Chamber of Commerce's magazine, called *Future*. It was my future too.

For Cadillac read it and asked me what I'd charge them if they reprinted five thousand copies. I said a penny a reprint.

They put my story into a black notebook and called it

Elmer's Little Black Notebook and printed five thousand, little realizing that these five thousand readers each knew at least ten hotel proprietors or butchers who were misbehaving and wanted to send them copies.

Cadillac then had to have fifty thousand printed, and sent me the one-cent royalty. Then Glenmore Distillers wanted reprints. I made the same deal: one cent for each reprint. This sounded small to them until they realized how many thousands of their readers wanted ten and even one hundred.

I rebilled myself with a new speaking title, "Take an Hour to Say No," and found that chambers and firms would listen to this speech on courtesy and politeness. I had been lucky enough to change and ride with the trend of the times.

My three points in the new and timely talk were:

1. Take an Hour to Say No.
2. Don't Ration Courtesy.
3. Look for Familiar Faces.

I hammered this speech across the country and back. I found it difficult at times to give my speech on politeness in certain hotels, especially when I told how ice served in hotel rooms now was eight hundred dollars a ton. (Figure it out yourself at fifty cents a bowl!)

I told how this angered so many guests that they swiped the glasses and "to make sure they wouldn't break, they wrapped them up in the hotel towels."

The hotel associations in certain states got after me.

Other hotel managers refused to let me give my speech in their hotels. Naturally this only highlighted the talk and made it as popular as a book banned in Boston.

Finally, the New York Hotel Association, through my friends at the Hotel Pennsylvania, had me give the speech in New York. They had the largest audience ever to hear a speaker there, for I was controversial with my new talk.

I can only say I got out alive, and had even more speaking engagements offered me.

Opportunity is all around us, if we will only listen for the knock. That's as corny a statement as a newspaperman ever made, but it is the corn that still sells today.

Your experiences are of value to the world, if you will learn the neat little art of getting them across to others.

4 WAYS TO WIN PEOPLE OVER

Rule 1:   Talk first about what you know best—Your own personal experiences.

Rule 2:   Talk to others in their own language.

Rule 3:   Make daily and excellent use of your mirror.

Rule 4:   Say something simple.

Put these to daily use, and you will find more happiness, more social success and greater business gains in life, regardless of who you are or what you do.

15

How to Speak Before Service Clubs

The ambition of many persons is to be able to stand up in front of a service club of local citizens and give a speech— and get away alive.

At least, get away without ridicule.

Let me pass on to you now some practical information on how to win over such an audience:

Rule 1: Have a story to tell—tell it—then sit down

Now that sounds simple enough, but so many speakers have no story to tell. They stand up with a string of funny stories they read in *Reader's Digest,* and try to get away with these yarns.

Or they try to discuss something they are not expert in.

Service clubs seldom expect whirlwind speakers. Most clubs never pay their local speakers, and so can't expect to have famous speeches delivered at their weekly meetings.

All they want is a half-hour of interest.

So stand up. Tell your experiences—your adventures. Tell them about the new plant that is coming to town and what it will mean to them. Tell them about your new product, your ideas for improving the city, a home, a back yard.

Start right off with the meat of your talk. Don't have a long-winded lead-up to your talk. Start off by saying something startling, such as: "Fifty people in town will die this year from rabies."

Start off in headline language. You have their full attention, for they or their families might be one of the fifty.

Now go into the facts of what you have said. Sum up. Ask for action. Then sit down with some final dramatic statement such as: "Will your child be the next to die? Prevent this by using the plan I just outlined!"

Say your piece. Say it well and short. Then sit down.

Rule 2: Tell them the things they want to hear

Too often people make use of service clubs to push some pet hobby, idea, or farfetched scheme that is of no interest to members of their audience. This is a big mistake. Ask yourself: Will others be interested in how I catch butterflies? Will others want to hear what is wrong with sewers in my part of town? Will others be interested in how ants build their anthills in South Africa?

Put your speech to this test.

If you feel others will want to hear you on such subjects, then fine. You are all set and the chances of gaining your audience's attention are good.

Rule 3: Give a lot of "for examples" in your speech

You are convinced that what you have to say is of major interest to the particular gathering in front of you. You are clever enough to talk gardening to the ladies club and selling to the salesmanship club.

Now give examples. Make a statement, then use a "for example." Say: "For example, the other day a mailman was bitten by a rabid dog and died. If we had a leash law, this man's life would have been saved."

Give many examples and proof too. Say: "For instance, a child got lost the other day and wandered away from home. Fortunately a neighbor had her dog leashed up and it could not reach the child. Two days later the dog was declared rabid. That's an example of what might have happened to your own child."

People like to have examples. It proves your point. So learn how to fill your talk with "for examples" and "for instances."

Rule 4: Always explain why you chose your subject

Have you ever walked away from a speech wondering, "Why did he talk on that subject?" "What was he trying to get across anyway?"

78

The speaker had failed to tell you why he was talking on the Rabid Dog Situation in Town. He left you wondering why he, of all people, should discuss such a situation before a Lion's Club.

But he might have made this clear by saying: "I'm a parent myself. I have children, like yours, who might be bitten by a rabid dog. That is why I am standing before this group and asking that they do something about it."

He might even go further and say: "The reason I have chosen the Lion's Club to tell my story is that they are progressive. They get things done, and I truly hope once you hear my story and see what is to be done, that you people will do it."

You are explaining why you are there; why you are speaking on this subject; why you are speaking before this particular audience, and not before the city council where the leash law would have to be made finally.

Rule 5: Don't stand like an iron dog on a lawn

The platform is no place for a poker face. Keep the poker face for the card table.

When you are in front of the audience, smile. The monkey-see, monkey-do instinct moves the audience, and they'll smile back at you.

Remember, the cigar store Indian never sold a cigar. All he did was get you into the store where a bright young fellow with a pleasant smile sold you a two-for-a-quarter Bering

79

Cigar instead of a nickel one by saying, "Look—it won't unravel in the mouth while smoking!"

So move around as much as the microphone will allow. If you move too much you'll walk out of "voice distance" of the mike. If this is your habit, get a microphone that hangs around your neck.

Use gestures—long and large ones, for they look normal to the last row. Talk high; talk low. Make your voice as interesting as your words. People like good delivery as well as a good message.

Rule 6: Have gimmicks and gadgets

Keep the eyes as well as the ears of the listeners occupied. Pull out gimmicks that amuse, new gadgets that dramatize your message. Make use of visual aids, but no graphs and charts or mimeographed material.

For example, startle your audience by showing them a dog's skull, saying: "Here is the skull of a dog that was declared rabid only last week!"

Hold up a picture of a neighborhood with dogs and kids and say: "Here is a picture, which you can look at later on, of a neighborhood that may be your own. You will note ten children and five dogs. Will one of these dogs be rabid?"

That's dramatic talking, perhaps a little hard-hitting, but proper for a speaker who really wants to sell his audience on a civic project.

80

Rule 7: Talk to them—don't give them a lecture

People don't want to go to a noonday luncheon and be given a lecture. They want to hear somebody talk on something of amusement, interest or value to them.

Never point a finger at an audience—for four other fingers are pointing back at you. Gesture widely, with the flat of the hand. Never finger-point in schoolroom and lecture fashion.

Never scold the audience. Have fun with them if you want, but never say: "It is your fault that we must have a leash law in the first place, because if you were alert fathers you'd have all your dogs vaccinated and this rabid situation would never have developed."

Talk—don't orate to an audience.

Say something simple. Then sit down. Let your message do the job!

Rule 8: Don't have distracting mannerisms

Don't attract attention to yourself with mannerisms that annoy people. Don't scratch your nose constantly. Don't run your fingers through your hair. Never tap a constant finger on the table—or the microphone. Don't sway back and forth—you'll make the audience dizzy. Avoid any constant movement of the body, face, mouth or arms.

Keep your arms at your side until you decide to use them to prove a point. Put hands in your pockets if that is natural with you. Lean on the podium if you wish, but don't slouch over it.

Avoid loud clothes. Sell yourself, not your tailor.

Never rustle papers in front of the sensitive ears of the microphone, and avoid drinking water. You'll get a captive audience so thirsty they can't wait until you are finished so they also can have a drink.

Be natural, as though you were in a room of friends; but don't talk with a smoke in your hands.

On certain occasions in an informal group, sit on the desk if you wish, but seldom at a noonday service club. It's too informal.

Watch your mannerisms and they'll watch out for you. Use your mirror to find these mannerisms, then avoid them.

Rule 9: Don't emphasize every word you say

A book filled with too many italics and capital letters loses its effect, and the same with the speaker who punches each line.

Save your punches for the words you really want to get across. Soften others.

Often a low-spoken word that comes out suddenly has more real wallop than one that is shouted.

The loud speaker, all gestures, all shouts, soon loses his audience. It fails to hear him any more than the soldier hears loud gunshots after he has heard the first dozen or so.

Let your words match your thoughts. When you talk about a fiercely rabid dog, make the words fierce-sounding. When you talk about a poor child who has been bitten, soften the words.

Then when you ask for help—ASK FOR IT in capital letters.

Rule 10: Don't have a dozen anticlimaxes

Once you have raised your audience to a high pitch, stop —sit down—quit! Too often the hands of an audience are ready to applaud, only to have you keep right on going. You keep right on driving home point after point. You are overselling the audience.

They wanted to buy what you had to say ten minutes ago —but you kept right on going until they started to yawn or look at their watches. Then it was too late.

You had too many anticlimaxes.

Rule 11: Ask them to do something

The talk is over but if you failed to end by asking for action, it has been a waste of time.

It is like a salesman getting you excited about an insurance policy, then saying as he walks off, "Think about what I had to say, will you?"

Ask for action. When you have finished tell them what to do, what must be done, or what you advise them to do. Say: "You have my story on the rabid situation in this town. You, the Lions, can do two things:

"One, you can back up a publicity campaign to have all dogs vaccinated.

"Two, you can start a publicity campaign for a leash law.
"Which plan do you want?

"I highly recommend that you form a committee as soon as I sit down, to search for ideas on how to sell this community on dog vaccinations so that our children can still play with their dogs and the dogs can still have freedom.

"Which of you will now stand up and offer to head this committee?"

That's asking for definite action. That's showing the way to what you want done.

16

Be Yourself on the Platform

One day I had an interesting proposal made to me.

DuMont Television came to me and offered, at no cost, to put twenty minutes of my fifty-minute "Selling the Sizzle" speech into an all-color movie providing they reserved the right to use it first with all salesmen of television products. I could then rent it to other groups.

The idea intrigued me. My message, now given close to five thousand times and soon to equal the number of times Dr. Russell Conwell gave his talk on "Acres of Diamonds," could be given before thousands instead of hundreds.

On the same night, my experiences and adventures in helping others make a living through better selling methods could be shown in a hundred cities.

I gladly worked out the program with Dr. DuMont, Dan Halpin, Cal Affleck and others of DuMont, and set about making the movie.

I was asked to put my thoughts into a twenty-minute

manuscript, which I did. It was then sent to a professional writer and he put it into script form, and the actors were hired to support me—and my troubles began.

I became tongue-tied once more.

Ever stand up in front of a camera, with electricians all around you, a script girl, a director, an assistant director, and try to say something you have memorized?

Actually, I could not even say, "He's a DuMont dealer," in a normal voice. You think that silly? Then let me tell you there are twelve ways of saying, "I never said he stole money." Say the sentence in front of a mirror and highlight the first word as you say the sentence. Then the second word as you say it again, and when you have repeated the sentence six times you will have emphasized six different words and have gotten six different meanings.

Now repeat the same sentence, again emphasizing a different word each time, but letting your voice end in a question mark. You will then have six more different meanings— or a total of twelve meanings for the one sentence.

So I ask you, how many ways can you say, "He's a DuMont dealer"? It took me two hours that day just to say those lines the right way.

It is a great experience speaking before a microphone. It is a greater experience in front of a camera.

The only advice I can give is to be as natural as possible. Learn the meanings of your lines instead of the actual words, then stand up and deliver your lines.

For example, in giving my first Wheelerpoint in selling, "Don't Sell the Steak—Sell the Sizzle," I am told not to memorize it, just to give it as I would on the platform.

I am then put in front of the camera and told to talk. I do. But I am only halfway through when someone hollers, "Cut." A light bulb has blown out. It is fixed. I again start off. This time an airplane goes by. "Cut" again. I start all over. And after doing this same bit for an hour or so, it is declared okay, and we proceed on to more lines.

I am told it often takes a full day of this sort of "shooting" just to get three minutes of finished movie product.

Try to be natural, too, when posing for pictures taken by the press or by the speaking committee. Always let the cameraman do the posing he wants. Let him be the boss, and you'll come out looking fine; but fight him, and you'll see one of those pictures next day in the newspaper that makes you look like a dictator, with your mouth wide-open.

I have seldom hated a person who smiled when he told me I was wrong or asked me to do something, for his smile took the place of a thousand extra words.

Learn to smile at people. At cameras.

Walk toward a podium with a ready smile, a brisk walk—and watch the audience respond when you say, "Let me tell you my experiences with the headhunters of South Africa."

In our training schools part of our voice drilling is to say the following lines, with facial expressions and voice tones to back them up:

87

> Elmer had a little steak: (*smile*)
> He liked it not at all—(*scowl*)
> But when they put the sizzle in, (*surprise*)
> He ate the plate and all! (*big grin!*)

Try that in front of your mirror and watch your facial expressions to make sure you are training yourself to use appropriate inflections for each thought, and right facial expressions to back them up.

Here is another good voice drill:

> Sing a song of sixpence, (*smile*)
> A pocketful of whizzles, (*quizzical look*)
> Four and twenty prospects (*raised brows*)
> All enjoying sizzles. (*happy expression*)

These sound silly, but it is amazing how they will work in helping you put expression into your face, so that the next time you tell a funny story in the lounge or on the platform, you will find people unconsciously imitating your expression and riding along with your story. People dislike stone faces. They like warm faces. Faces that react to thoughts being given. Voices that have the meaning of the thoughts.

Here is another little ditty I picked up to lower the voice, for somehow the low voice seems to carry more weight than a high, screechy voice:

> Fifteen men on a dead man's chest:
> Yo, ho, ho and a bottle of rum.

As I say the second line, I start bending my knees until I get my voice to go right down to the floor with me.

Probably you aren't planning to make a movie, but if you do, remember the advice given here. You can use it facing a camera at a picnic or at a press conference, at a sales meeting or in the neighbor's back yard.

17

You Can't Erase the Spoken Word

As a reporter, if I said the wrong thing, I could erase it. In the event I failed to erase it and it passed by me, then there was the copyman who would check me. Often an editor over him.

There was always a check-guard against my words written on paper. But spoken words have no check-guards.

You say them and they fly into the world to bring people joy or anger, to build up the spirits of people or to tear them down.

Words that fly like daggers; words that flutter like feathers.

Learn the art of thinking twice before saying a thing once. Weigh each word well. Then if you still feel it may be misunderstood, search for another word. You can't erase the spoken word.

Hesitate before you ridicule, find fault, alibi or make excuses, and the chances of saying the wrong words will be cut in half. Then "think twice, speak once" when you discuss politics, religion or any sensitive subject. In such cases, it might be best to write down what you have to say, let others read it, then do a lot of self-editing. If still in doubt, read the part of your message that might be misunderstood. Don't gamble on putting in a single extemporaneous word that may be misquoted.

You can say, "He is a fine *man*" or you can say, "He is a *fine* man!" The tone of your voice will tell you which is complimentary and which is filled with sarcasm.

Words spoken with tinges of sarcasm, impatience, annoyance, are words best left alone, since your tone of voice can't be erased either.

Some tones annoy. Others please.

The live television show is filled with goofs and fluffs, because again the spoken word cannot be erased or eliminated. This is why so many prefer the filmed TV shows, for then the fluffs can be eliminated as they are in the movies.

On the platform you are handicapped. You can't erase a joke that was better left unsaid. You can't erase that tone of voice that you flung out into the room, that darted here, stabbed there.

To prevent saying the wrong thing, try not to speak extemporaneously. If you have gotten a story, a message down pat, then don't gamble with it. It is so much easier to change the audience than to change the speech.

Struggle for perfection. Then stick to the tested material you have. You won't be gambling on whether they'll laugh, or whether they will misunderstand.

18

To Win an Audience, First Conquer Yourself

Before you conquer an audience, before you conquer a house party—you must first conquer your own fears and anxieties and worries, and so be clear to conquer other things.

If you yourself are weak, hesitant, then you will not have the power to command and conquer others. A doctor with acne is a bad one to go out and give advice on curing that ailment in others.

I am trying to get one thing across to you as a potential public speaker, or as a mediocre speaker who wants to be a better one, and to you who just want to side-step your inferiority complexes and be able to carry on a suitable conversation with a few friends.

The one thing is this: Rid yourself of your mental ailments. Of anxieties, worries and a defeatist attitude.

You can't win others over if you are struggling with your

own weaknesses. First get rid of your own weaknesses, then you are cleared and able to win over others.

GETTING RID OF FEARS

Most fears are bogiemen. Once the light is turned on in a room, they prove to be only big chairs and stools and benches. Not any more than that. Fear that you haven't the education to carry on a conversation with others is all wrong. Education is merely a knowledge of something that you excel in.

Maybe it is pie-making, maybe dressmaking; maybe the movies, ball games, the books you read. You do excel in something. Just find that. It is about you somewhere if you'll only look for it.

Maybe you have a knowledge of something that others do not have. Maybe you are outstanding because of your fine married life, because your garden is rid of insects, or because your car is the best-kept one in the neighborhood.

You are educated in that subject and in that subject you don't have fear, and so you can hold attention.

GETTING RID OF ANXIETY

You are sweating out a speech. You are nervous. You are concerned that you may not go over, but even more concerned that you will forget what you have to say.

You won't read the speech, so you are afraid you'll forget what you have to say.

The cure for this anxiety is to realize one thing: *What*

you don't say they won't miss.

Only you know what you have left out, so why let this anxiety upset your talk? Give it. Talk to your friends around the garden party; talk at the noonday lunch, the big banquet.

Rid yourself of such anxieties. If you have anxieties before a party, a dance, a banquet, a lecture, your delivery will suffer. You will stammer and stutter, hem and haw. You will fail to conquer because you haven't conquered your own anxieties.

Getting Rid of Worry

Worry eats into the soul like acid. People can sense a worrier when he starts to talk. Somehow or other his eyes aren't entirely on you. He is inclined to hem. Then to haw. He shifts around. He bites his lips. He taps his fingers.

He is nervous because he is worried about something.

Perhaps he is woried that the audience won't like him, that he isn't dressed properly for the affair. That he is "out of place," that he is among people that outclass him.

He worries and in worrying he spoils his chances to win over others.

This person must realize people will like him for what he is, not for what he thinks he should be. They will like him most if he talks on a subject he is familiar with, or simply becomes their best listener while they talk. People will forget your dress, your need of a haircut. They will forget the fact that you may not be financially equipped as they are.

For people will overlook anything but a poor conversationalist—a bore.

Learn how to converse, and you will never be out of place. Learn how to talk with others, and they'll never consider you a bore. Learn the art of being interesting, and people will forget the size of your bankbook or the cut of your clothes.

Before you try to conquer the Friday Night Bridge Club, before you try to conquer the Downtown Kiwanis Club, before you have ambitions to go to the Big City and repeat a Horatio Alger, set about conquering your own weaknesses.

Take a sheet of paper, like I did once, and write down your fears, your anxieties and your worries.

List as many as you can. The more the merrier, for the sooner you get them on paper, in daylight, the sooner you will have isolated them, and can find cures for them.

Now opposite each weakness, mark down the cure as you see it. Be honest with yourself. If your weakness is a lack of vocabulary, then bone up on the dictionary. Or listen to a few speakers and be convinced a large vocabulary isn't necessary. If your fear or anxiety is lack of education, then find out wherein you excel. Find something you do better than others if it is only mowing a lawn, then talk so well about your experiences mowing a lawn that the neighbors come over and admire it.

Banish your personal fears, anxieties and worries. Conquer yourself—then you can conquer any group in the entire world.

19

Eleven Ways to Test Your Speech

You can't always win. You can't always sell your ideas to others, no matter how closely you follow the book rules.

I have had many flops and duds on the platform, especially on new speeches, or when I forgot my regular pattern and tried to pull in new and strange ideas that were not tested or were out of my line. I have learned to test my stories, jokes and ideas on small friendly groups before I let them loose before large paying audiences.

At times I have failed to heed my own advice. I have tried out new stories and new ideas, finding they didn't sound so good in front of an audience as they did in my mind. If I had given them the "mirror test," I'd perhaps never have used half of these new ideas.

So I say welcome a few defeats. They show you what not to do the next time. Let me pass on to you now six ways you can go about losing the "sale" to an audience. If you ever flop in getting yourself across with others, put your speech to this test:

Why I Lost My Audience

1. *I talked over their heads.* I let erudite information get the better of me. I was over their heads, and they asked for my head.

2. *I showed intellectual impatience.* I was too far ahead of my audience and when they didn't catch up with my ideas, I became obviously impatient with them. They got real impatient with me too.

3. *I acted superior to my audience.* I knew I was good, but I let the audience know I knew. Then they suddenly felt superior to me.

4. *I got antagonistic to the audience.* I used sarcasm. I let my voice stab them. I resented their resentment and they knew it, and I found myself talking to myself.

5. *I lacked knowledge of what I was talking about.* I was egged on into talking on subjects I was inexperienced in, and soon I found myself in deep water, then in hot water.

6. *I got long-winded from my success.* I went over, yes, but I should have quit long before I did. Instead, I let my success overpower me. I got long-winded and talked myself out of friends.

Once you have felt your speech was a flop, or your conversation with the group was a miserable failure, ask yourself the following:

DID I MAKE THESE MISTAKES IN DEALING WITH PEOPLE?

1. *I knocked my competitor (or friend).* I ran someone to the ground, not realizing what I was doing. I will never say bad things about those not present. I won't gossip.
2. *I high-pressured people.* I had a captive audience and took advantage of it by overly pressuring them. I should have been less forceful, less pugnacious. I must use question marks more than crowbars.
3. *I was far too egotistical.* I talked "I," "I," "I." I never let others do some of the talking while I merely listened. I must learn to be a good listener first, a good talker second—and quit bragging.
4. *I lacked confidence.* I let fear get hold of me. My audience sensed I lacked confidence in my ideas, my thought, my words. So they walked away from me, lacking confidence in me.
5. *I failed to demonstrate.* I could have shown a dog collar, a vaccination certificate, a leash, and made my talk more visual and less wordy. I must learn that a demonstration takes the place of ten minutes of conversation.

Train yourself to find the causes of your mistakes. Ask friends for their advice.

Above all, ask your enemies. For they will perhaps give you your best help by telling you your greatest weakness. You often learn more from your enemies than from your friends, from your severest critics than from your warmest supporters.

Don't be downhearted at your mistakes. Don't let them upset you, or bring back that old feeling of defeat, inferiority or worry and anxiety.

20

How to Make People
Buy Your Ideas

When you are carrying on a conversation with someone,
when you are planning a speech or a lecture, remember this:

PEOPLE WANT THESE THINGS

Health
More time
Money
Prestige
Success
Authority
Recognition
Influence
Popularity
Education

Improvement

Less Work

Frame your words and your appeals to strike one of the "inner motives" in people, and they'll give you their undivided attention.

Here now are some more ways to make people say "Yes":

People Buy Your Ideas Because

1. They want personal gains.
2. They desire love.
3. They want to live forever.
4. They want to be "he-men."
5. They want adventure.

Now if you want three more excellent pointers to win over others in a group of two or two hundred, remember the following:

3 Points to Success

1. *People buy for self-preservation.* First in life they want food, clothing, shelter, protection. Show them how you can satisfy this first need in their lives.
2. *People buy next for romantic purposes.* Once they have security they want luxury. Better things. Bigger cars. Trips. Adventure. They want life. Show them how to get these things.
3. *People want money.* They must have money to get self-preservation and romance, so show them how

102

what you have to offer will get them money or save them money—to make their daydreams possible through financial security.

It is an old rule that you must make people thirsty before they will buy your product, service or platform idea. Put this formula we used in our training schools to good use in your next contact with people.

How to Make 'Em Thirsty

1. *Don't make 'em drink—make 'em thirsty.* Present your case so well, they will lean toward you, not bend away. Lead others, don't drive them.
2. *Don't sell an empty box.* Promise all you can but when you deliver, give them more than they bargained for. Give them the baker's dozen, the free lollipop that brings them back.
3. *If you can't convince 'em—join 'em.* When you see some person or persons balking you, back up a little. You can't convince a balky person but you can join with him long enough to start swaying him back to your way of thinking.

In dealing with people you must understand their desires, hopes, ambitions and daydreams. Their fears, their worries and their anxieties all are important to you since they tell you how to frame your words to win them over to your way of thinking.

The more you understand people, the more you will know

what to say and do to get them over to your way of thinking.

Knowing a man fears having his child bitten by a mad dog prompts you to use that fear in saying, "Let us do away with rabid dogs. Your child may be next."

Knowing a man likes more leisure, you say, "You will find this method one that will give you five extra hours a week in leisure time."

If you realize a man wants security, then talk security; if he wants adventure, then paint him a great adventure story in what you are trying to put across to him.

Remember, too, in order to make people like you, you must first like people.

21

How to Banish Nervousness

I have asked speakers, "What do you do to get the butter-flies out of your stomach before you speak?" I have asked famous actors and actresses the same thing as I worked with them on their publicity in the Eastman Theatre.

Each has given me his or her pet cure, his or her system to overcome the nervousness that often comes over a person just before he steps onto a stage or a platform. Each has told me personal methods to keep anxiety off the podium or stage.

Before I stand up, I often feel a shiver run through me. I have all sorts of thoughts running rampant, such as, "Will I go over this time? Will they quiet down? Will they like what I have to say?"

I would like to pass on to you the many tips, suggestions, aids and advice given me by professional speakers and those of the stage. In their advice I am sure you will find one or more "cures" for your own worries in meeting or facing strangers.

I believe that the best cure-all to overcome butterflies in the stomach, nervousness and anxiety in talking to strangers is: *Take three big breaths before you speak*. I have tried this myself. In so doing I have given my lungs oxygen, and I have slowed down my pulse, quieted my nerves, and supplied air inside of me to back up my words.

"Just take three breaths before you speak," said David Rubinoff to me one time. "It helps me especially since I have something of a dialect. But the oxygen seems to fill my lungs and scare out fear."

The next time you are about to enter an office or a roomful of people, or step up on a podium, or merely stand up in front of an audience to bow, take three breaths.

Then note the composure that comes over you. The poise that suddenly comes to you. And watch how easily the words flow out of your mouth.

I have also tried this often and know it works: concentrating my gaze on a friendly face in the audience.

As you stand up, the audience looks at you. They don't know you. So they just look at you, and seeing a flood of faces staring up at you has frightened many a person.

I find that seeking out a familiar face helps me overcome my fear. The friendly or familiar face does one more thing for me. It helps me concentrate on my talk. It keeps my mind from worrying about whether I am going over. It warms me up.

One warning: Don't stare too long at one face or the face will become nervous, and others in the audience will look at the person you keep staring at. So pick out many people to look at. Many friendly or familiar faces.

Then as the talk warms up, and you gain confidence and composure, let your eyes rove all over the place, and don't forget the head table. Look at them occasionally to let them know you know they are still there.

When you look at a person squarely in the face, that person feels all your words are for him! Watch him brighten up. Watch him become a booster of yours.

Here Are Some Random Ways to Banish Fears

I'd like to pass on some other tips to help you become a better talker with friends or a better speaker before groups.

Pause for poise

Pauses help you get your breath. Help the audience to absorb your thoughts. Learn to pause occasionally, so long as the pauses aren't long, drawn-out. Learn the art of verbal commas, periods, exclamation points. Learn how to pause before an important statement—how to emphasize that statement—by a pause after you have given it.

Avoid "ahs" and "ers"

Remove the whiskers from your words. Take off the fuzz. Pause on and off, but don't lead into a pause or end a pause with a long "ah" or an "er." Another word to avoid is the word "and-a." As Richard Borden has said, "I take a hammer, and every time I use 'and-a' in practicing a talk I hit the desk. Often I hit my finger. But it breaks me of the habit."

Don't trail-off your sentences

Learn how to stop at the end of a thought. How to put a period at the end of each idea. Avoid trailing-off each sentence with a meaningless phrase. Clip the sentences with periods. Say it once, then stop. Avoid word garbage.

Don't strike poses

Will Rogers chewed gum and kept his hands in his pockets and never used a comb, just his hand to push back his hair. But he had platform poise. He had character. He didn't strike false poses. He didn't assume dramatic postures. Be your own good self in front of others.

Watch your speed of delivery

The professors of speech tell me an audience can absorb up to 150 words a minute and still get your meaning, and can listen down to about 90 words a minute without becoming bored. The idea in holding interest is to talk fast until you get to a big, main point—then highlight it by slowing down your gait. Make this your rule:

Maximum speed limit. . . . . 150 words per minute
Minimum speed limit. . . . . 90 words per minute

6 STEPS TO SUCCESSFUL SPEAKING

Step 1: Knowing you are good makes you good.
Step 2: Don't bluff your way.
Step 3: Never tell experts how to do their job.
Step 4: Don't sound pedantic!
Step 5: Let them hear your ideas—and not you.
Step 6: Have something to say.

22

A Sure Cure for Platform Fears

Here is what my experiences addressing audiences in Mexico and in Canada taught me about conquering fear and learning how to understand different types of audiences.

Now in Canada you will find the ultimate in courtesy. They will meet you at the plane or train regardless of the hour, and they are very keen at knowing when to leave you after breakfast, when to pick you up again, and they respect your wishes, desires and sight-seeing interests.

You will find a Canadian audience accustomed to listening to speeches, willing to give you the fullest opportunity to speak—but just as willing to give you sound criticism as applause. You will always know where you stand with a Canadian audience.

One of the finest traits they have is to ask one of the

audience (picked in advance) to stand up after the talk and "thank the speaker." This chap then takes up to five minutes to review your talk, comment on it, and in so doing, thank you by letting you know he has heard each word and is benefiting by your advice.

Because of their own abilities to talk they appreciate your abilities. One coal miner can recognize another in a hurry. One oil man likes to talk things over with another oil man. Speakers usually like appreciative audiences, and the most appreciative audience (though the most critical, perhaps) is one made up of amateur speakers.

I would say welcome a trip to any Canadian city to speak. You will add to your experience on the platform, you will learn a lot about the courtesies of handling a speaker, and you will come out a better speaker. You may be told frank things that are as hard to take as some medicines. But if you realize that you benefit from suggestions more than pats on the back, you will emerge a greater talker.

You will emerge, too, a greater conversationalist for you will probably be hobnobbing with Canadians in suites, bars, homes, clubs. Here you will learn a great deal about the art of conversation as practiced by the Canadians, many of whom are from English and Scottish stock (not to forget the Irish), and were born with the gift of self-expression.

You will gain knowledge of how to carry on a pleasant conversation. You will learn the art of being a good listener first, a good talker second.

111

Lastly, you will find the best audience in the world for your amusing stories, yarns, tall tales of your own experiences and adventures; a polite audience too, which, if you aren't alert, you will unconsciously take advantage of by being "too American" and forgetting when to stop and let a Canadian take over.

I advise a speaking trip to Canada to anyone really wanting to learn the arts and sciences of platform speaking—and how to be a good listener.

I believe the farther south you go the more emotional people become.

The Mexican audience will applaud you, shout boos, shout bravos. There will be for you an *ole*, a *viva*, a cheer; or they will hiss you audibly if you are bad.

They react in a hurry. Their hearts control their heads. If they like you they will give you an *abrazo*, and put their arms around you. They want to shake hands several times during an evening. They are warm of heart and hand.

Tip: Refer to them as South Americans, yourself as a North American. All on this continent are Americans!

If they like what you are saying, it is nothing for them to toss their hats into the air. It is nothing for them to toss bottles at you if they don't like you. They are truly emotional and make a great audience for a speaker with the spirit to go to Mexico and test out his skill.

If he does he will learn one thing: that his gestures and facial expressions will be watched more closely than in

Canada. A Canadian will at times close his eyes as he rests his head on his hand, thinking about your words. A Mexican never takes his eyes off you.

Thus a Mexican can detect a phony through his eyes—while a Canadian is more apt to discover a phony through his ears.

In Mexico you jump around. Move about. Raise the hands. Lower them. An outsider might well think you were angry, but you are only making those large emotional gestures to inspire your audience to action.

In Canada you may talk with fewer windmill effects, although a Canadian will, at times, like some dramatic gestures, some bursts of emotion. They rouse him off his elbow —but he won't like an entire meeting of such gestures. The Mexican never stops wanting action.

Incidentally, 65 per cent of an audience of businessmen in Mexico will understand English.

One thing I learned about fear of meeting people, of standing up on strange platforms, is to accept the fear at its worst!

I have learned that often the best part of a journey is the planning of it all winter long. Once the journey starts it seems to be so full that it is over before you know it. The planning occupies a longer time and so often gives greater pleasure.

Now with fears the same psychological factor takes place. You have your greatest fears before and not during a session with people. You fear for days speaking at a sales convention; you fear for hours talking to the boss, the employees, some friends.

You die a thousand deaths *before* the event. Then when it happens, it happens so quickly that actually you don't have time to fear.

I would like to say that, based on this reportorial observation, it is best to accept fear. Accept the worst in fear. Accept the greatest of anything that can happen to you, but accept it in advance.

Sit back and figure you will forget your speech, that the audience will walk out on you. That they will boo and jeer you. Accept the worst. Live it up. Then sit back and say, "Well, that is over with. Now let me think about what I'll say!"

This psychosomatic idea is an old one, they tell me. That is, it is a real science of words over body. That if you will go through all your fears beforehand, then nothing is left.

Fear as much as you want. Then sit back, relax and say, "The worst that can happen is over with. I am free of fear."

Or sit back and say, "So what! They can always walk out on me when I tell a funny story, but what is so wrong about that? I will still be alive and will still be on hand."

The worst that can happen is—well, what? All they can say is you flopped, and no one will send you to jail, hang you or tar and feather you. So what have you lost? Nothing, if you are a good loser. You have gained an adventure not offered others, and will be greater by having had that adventure.

I think it was Lin Yutang who said that once you accept the worst that can happen to you under a given circumstance, you then have nothing left to do but relax and forget. In so relaxing, your mind is clear to think.

So face the worst calamity you can think will happen to you when you attend that party the boss is giving for his employees. Face this—then you'll have peace of mind providing you agree that the worst is over with and you don't give a hang now what they say or do about you.

It is sort of sticking out your chin and saying, "So what!"

You can't think sanely if your mind is loaded with fears, worries and anxieties about what will happen to you when you start to say, "Let me tell you about my experiences raising chickens. . . ."

The worst has already happened to you—right in your own home.

Emotions of fear, hate, despair, frustration, all will destroy you if you keep them sealed up. So release them, but in your own privacy. Live the deaths in your own home. Free your soul of these emotions, then go on the platform or to the meeting and be "fear-less."

Accept the worst and then you can go forward rid of worries!

The worst that can happen is that you may be toughened and hardened and made a better person.

23

The Art and Science
of Handling People

People are great teachers. They will educate you if you let
them and if you are tolerant and patient with their whims,
fancies and demands.

I never had the courage in the early days to argue with
people. So I had to listen and in listening, I profited.

Let me tell you what I've picked up from others in the
past nineteen years on the best ways to sell yourself to
others, whether a wife, a husband, the barbecue crowd on
Saturday night, or a big banquet when they are ready to
turn the gavel over to you as the new president.

Here are four steps to sell yourself to others:

Step 1: SUGGEST—don't shove!

It is not well to issue orders to employees, family or an
audience. Show them the way, if you want, but make it possible for them to follow you without being obviously shoved.

Shove with tactful sales appeals and the dangling of fun, joy, profit—a sizzle—in front of their noses, but don't heave-ho at people.

"How does this strike you?" is much better than "I know this is what you should have!" The question mark again versus the crowbar.

Learn to lead people—try not to shove or push them.

Step 2: "No" turned around spells "on"

It is often necessary to hear the word "no," or feel the word "no" from a mass audience, before you can win. That is, providing you will realize one thing, that a "no" turned around means "on."

Just as "now" turned around means "won."

So you must often turn a friend or a group of strangers completely around before they will say "Yes."

Once you have people so stirred up they are awake and aroused enough to say "No," then you know you have a chance. It's the group that sits sleepily on its hands that never say "Yes."

So learn how to stir up people enough for them to say "No," so you can turn it around and get them "on" the band-wagon for you!

Step 3: Leave 'em SMILING—not frowning!

A good vaudeville show leaves 'em laughing. You leave 'em laughing or smiling, or at least happy and joyful they spent the time with you.

117

The big trick is to save your best for the close, and wind it up in a big walloping ending.

George M. Cohan was a master of this art. His show may have been weak, but in his finale, the girls wore less, they waved more American flags, the orchestra played loudest, and the show ended happily.

Learn how to end dramatically. My trick is to do it with a humorous story at which they burst out laughing before I finish, and so I sit down in the middle of laughter.

Step 4: Talk WEDDINGS—not funerals

Don't be a wet blanket. Forget the world's troubles when you enter a room of people. Forget your own ailments and operations. Learn the art of talking weddings, not funerals.

People love weddings. They are sad at funerals.

No one cares about the sore throat you had before you came to the platform, or the fact you nearly lost a plane connection.

People want to hear about happiness—not troubles.

If they have troubles, then show them the way to happiness by following your program. Lead them to a better life.

Use these four steps yourself to win over others. To sell yourself to others. To help people and in so doing, help yourself to a better life.

Just remember some people like their apple peeled, others want it sliced; some like it in pies and others as applesauce;

118

so learn their tastes, then serve the apple the way they like it.

Don't force them to eat the apple the way you want to eat it. Learn in advance the way they like to enjoy their apples, then show them the way to own a crate of apples instead of just a bagful.

Remember that old rule of giving them more than they planned on: the baker's dozen! It is a mistake to put the shiny apples on the top, then let them find shoddy ones below the surface.

It is a mistake to cheat them out of a single apple. Let them find more than they bargained for, and you'll gain more than you bargained for.

24

How Words Saved
a Man's Life

This is perhaps as strange a "textbook" on the art of speaking, getting along with people, and overcoming fear of being with people as you'll ever read.

However, I have tried to fill these pages of my trials and disappointments in my climb up the ladder of speaking success with helpful rules, hints and suggestions to help every man, woman or youth who has yearned to be an interesting storyteller.

I have tried to analyze each of my own failures, get a rule from each downfall, so that you could have this rule and prevent your own defeats and make your own life happier.

Take, for example, two incidents in my life wherein a defeat, properly handled, finally became a victory.

My German and Irish ancestors gave me a liking for food, and with so many Navy E Award banquets during the war, and so many conventions right after the war, I began to stack on even more weight.

One day the Marines called me back and when the doctor took one look at me he turned to a group of Marines sitting on a bench playing checkers between wars, and said: "Look what peacetime did to a Marine!"

I was so mad, on the way home, that I ate three candy bars, a package of peanuts, and drank five soft drinks.

When I arrived home I found my wife had put in twin beds. "How come," I asked, "after all these years we now have twin beds?"

"Have you looked at yourself sidewise, lately?" she said. "You need a bed all by yourself."

I got so mad I went on a diet.

I began a study of what makes people fat, a study similar to my other one on what makes people buy. The war was over. Selling was still slow, and my story of courtesy and politeness was going downhill. It had petered out.

The more weight I lost, the more people gathered around to hear me tell them how I was losing it. Then suddenly it dawned on me, I had a new book and a new speech.

I tried to sell *The Fat Boy's Book* to my editors. Unfortunately for me, they were underfed and couldn't see a need in America for my book on diet.

I saw the need, though. I saw another trend, and wanted to join with the trend, and mustering up my best words and sales ideas into a story of fat in the Land of Plenty, I finally sold the editors on publishing the book.

I had gotten into their hair and they figured the best way to get me out was to publish 2,500 copies of the book. Then General Features Syndicate took hold and I ended up three years later with 250 newspapers carrying the Fat Boy story. I received 2,300,000 letters, which *Editor & Publisher* said broke an all-time record for any serial ever written in any newspaper.

There was another great event in my life. Another victory, but one that backfired.

It all happened one day at the Hotel Pennsylvania, now The Hotel Statler, in New York City when I had my office there in exchange for work I did for the hotel chain.

The manager telephoned me that a man was up on the roof threatening to jump off and did I have any magic words to prevent this.

This was a big assignment, but I went up with one of my assistants, a blonde named Diane Gregal.

I saw the situation in a hurry. Here was a man on the very roof's edge about to jump. Hundreds of police were there, firemen with nets, and eighty thousand spectators looking down on the hotel roof from office buildings everywhere.

I gulped. I had never stood in front of eighty thousand people before.

If the situation hadn't been one of saving a life, I'll bet you I'd have run off the roof in a hurry. But realizing the seriousness of the situation, I quickly asked what had been done up until then.

I was told a priest had tried to see the man and failed. That a rabbi had talked to the man about his family. That a doctor had tried to convince him he would surely die if he jumped, a policeman had told him he'd be pinched if he did and a fireman had said the jump was a long one to the net.

The man said nothing. I knew any word appeal by me, another man, would fail.

So I "sold dangerously."

Whenever you realize usual appeals will fail, and all seems lost anyway, you sometimes can succeed with bold, unexpected tactics. This is "selling dangerously."

I told Miss Gregal to go up to the man and cuss him out. To tell him, "Your wife is on the way from Brooklyn, and if she sees you in that ridiculous spot she'll sure tell you off in a hurry!"

The man reacted. He didn't seem to care if he was killed if he jumped. He didn't care much about anything, except one thing—his wife!

He thought of his wife seeing him in a ridiculous position and it was more than he could stand.

He walked off the roof!

Miss Gregal and I were front-page copy that night in New York newspapers, who hailed the "word magicians." I was a hero. Diane was a heroine!

Then suddenly some reporter had the idea this was a publicity stunt to sell the sizzle to the world. The papers turned on me. I was in disgrace for having used the poor man as a cheap publicity stunt to highlight our Tested Selling, Inc.

I was being condemned fast, until a week later the man again went up on the roof, and this time jumped to his death.

For years afterward, when someone was about to jump off a roof we were often called on to use our "magic words" to save him and in many cases we did.

25

How to Profit from Criticism

I always read what the Democrats say about the Republicans and what the GOP says about the followers of the donkey; for in so doing, I learn most about each.

In buying a new car I have found that the seller doesn't tell you the weak points of that car. He is too interested, too clever to tell you other than the fine points; but if you want to learn that car's weak points, then visit the competitor.

It is the same in life. If you want to hear nice things about yourself, then talk with your family and friends who are too kind to tell you your faults, or in liking you so well, don't ever see them.

Talking to friends is a mighty good way to build up your ego. It is great to hear your friends say, "That was a fine talk you gave last night. I liked the new stories you told."

It is wonderful to hear the wife say, "Joe, you were great tonight." It is a joy to hear the boss say, as he pats you on the arm, "You really put sizzle into that sales meeting today. I was proud of you."

It is a great uplift when people use those five magic words and say, "I am proud of you."

But does that teach you anything?

Will pats on the back and compliments strengthen you, or perhaps actually weaken you by covering up your errors until they have grown so big they are eating you away?

Isn't it often better to hear the bad news about cancer right at the start than to have someone try to cover it up until it is too late?

Wouldn't you like to hear about your faults, so you can improve yourself, as well as learn your good points so you can retain them?

I do appreciate compliments, but I benefit most from complaints.

I am always first to get out into the lobby after a talk, with my hat and coat on so I am not recognized, and then listen to the comments.

I learned this trick years ago in the theaters, during that spell when I was a movie critic and publicity man for Eastman Theatres and others in the Publix Theatres circuit.

I have noticed big artists in lobbies listening to comments. I have seen ushers required to stand in lobbies and mark down what people say as they leave.

Defeats help you. It is only fear of defeat that is harmful.

I highly recommend you eavesdrop on yourself. I know that people who listen at keyholes hear nothing kindly about themselves, but they learn what people dislike in them and then can improve themselves. It is well to know your weak points as well as your strong ones.

Remember, it is no disgrace to hear bad things about your-self. The disgrace is in doing nothing about them.

Here are some things your enemies might say about you:

"He's a phony." You pretended. You talked over your own head. You weren't honest. You assumed what you are not.

"He's a braggart." You talked too much about how good you were. The audience got tired of your aimless and point-less brags about yourself.

"He can't speak." You tried to orate and failed. Or you failed to abide by the standard rules of saying something simple, then proving the point, asking for the "order"—and sitting down. You violated too many good rules of conversation.

"He exaggerated too much." You talked millions instead of thousands. You were too fantastic in your statements. You tried to startle with outlandish remarks, but flopped instead.

"He sounded like a crackpot." Your idea was radical, which was all right; but you got too wound up, too darned serious about it. A light touch, some humor, a little wit—and per-haps you'd have sold the audience that you thought the idea great, and hoped they might agree with you, at least in part.

"He was a windbag." You made the great mistake of talk-

ing too long. You interpreted applause and smiles and laughter as a bid to keep right on talking beyond your time.

I have found the wisecracks of my enemies made me strong. I welcome their criticism. I'd appreciate them more perhaps if they were given to me as suggestions, but even as criticism, I always want to hear complaints.

If you listen to everybody, and in a kindly and acceptable manner, you will find your prayers coming true.

One last bit of advice on this subject: *Make the audience feel superior, not yourself.*

You always win when you make the other person in the room feel superior by inflating his ego—by not overexplaining everything you say, as if you felt, "This fellow is a dunce. I must explain it to him again."

One phrase I find most helpful in getting me across to others is, "I guess I didn't make myself quite clear. What I tried to say was . . ."

How much better this approach is to a person who doesn't get what you say, than to crack out, "You didn't get what I mean. Now let me repeat . . ."

I have found this magic way of handling people very effective.

VOICE SELF-TESTER

Want to gain more respect, confidence and attention when you stand up to "say a few words"?

Here are three ways to test out your own voice for volume, pitch, strength and attention-getting quality.

First, cup your hands behind your ears in radio-announcer fashion and then speak. In this way you can "hear" your own voice. You may be startled the first time you try this test.

Second, hold a V-shaped newspaper or open magazine a few inches in front of you and talk into it. The voice will bounce back to your ears and you will hear yourself as others hear you.

Third, stand in the corner of a room and speak up. The voice will hit the sides of the walls and return to your ears faster than if you spoke in the middle of a room.

Know how you sound to others. In this way you can improve the quality, texture and tone of your voice.

A voice that rings out properly, not too loudly, not too softly, gains the respect and attention of audiences; so make it a practice on and off to "hear" your own voice.

26

What Speaking Before 20,000 People Taught Me

Twenty thousand people had gathered at the request of the Dallas Chamber of Commerce, Jaycees, Sales Executives Club and other civic organizations to learn what they could about getting jobs and pulling faster out of the Depression.

The event was called the "Sales Mean Jobs" campaign. The idea was very simple—that every time a salesman makes a sale, some thirty-two workers behind him get a job replacing what was sold.

These are union figures and are quite true. For it took somebody to dig into the ground for the minerals to make the product, somebody to make the shovels, others to make the paint, the string, the paper, the tires on the trucks that delivered the item.

My assignment was to show these salespeople how to make more sales, to give them specific sales help and to inspire them to go out and ring the doorbells of business once more and help make the Depression history.

Ever stand up in front of twenty thousand faces?

You'll be amazed at the feeling you will have in your legs, in your throat, in your chest.

Twenty thousand people, and in a football bowl, with no ceiling but the stars, and no sounding boards to carry the voice! Your voice just leaves you and keeps right on going up to heaven, or wherever speakers' voices go when there aren't walls.

I had been taking some training in voice delivery. My voice was always slightly high. My problem, according to the experts, was to lower it by breathing from my stomach and not my chest.

Try this in front of the mirror. Breathe out from the diaphragm, then in. Note how you keep the throat clear of air, and find it hard to gag, become embarrassed due to lack of wind, or otherwise cause yourself needless troubles.

I knew I had to do one thing with these twenty thousand people—win their confidence.

If an audience detects insincerity you are whipped. If they feel you are pulling their leg, joshing them, making fun of them, treating them like twelve-year-olds—then they walk away from you mentally if not physically.

To win confidence, you must be sincere. To be sincere, you must be honest. Honesty is detected by an audience in a hurry.

131

I learned to talk to the heavens, to raise my head upward so that my face rose to the last row in the stadium, never to lower it and talk as though I had an audience of just a few people in the first row.

It seems that if you raise your face skyward, you look normal to those in the back row. You look as though you were really giving out. The high head holds attention in the very back row.

This audience was hungry for knowledge of what to do to get jobs or to make their jobs more productive.

There were factory workers and salesmen for baked goods; there were telephone operators, bankers, doctors, lawyers and a multitude of salespeople from the stores, all wanting to hear the story of "Selling the Sizzle."

It was a very important moment in their lives, and in mine too. It was my biggest dream to go over with twenty thousand in a stadium.

The experience taught me that to gain the confidence of an audience you must deserve it. That you must give them simple pointers, successful methods, and remove any hooey or attempts to bombast them into line. You must say something simple.

I told myself, here are twenty people many times multiplied, and I will talk to the twenty and tell them all I have to say; then I will go over with the other 19,980 people in front of me.

So I talked to twenty people. I told twenty people my experiences making people buy. I gave them the specific sizzles to sell underwear, shirts, cars, insurance policies, bicycles, bread, real estate. I told this to twenty people and the other 19,980 people heard it too.

The big test was on me. Would I again become tongue-tied? Had I lost my fear of people, or would this fear suddenly return when I looked at this mass of people, the largest ever gathered to hear a sales speaker?

I stood up. The audience became quiet. I spoke. My voice went out from my throat. It kept right on going. I didn't have the feel of walls to reflect my voice and bolster it up. It just kept right on going and going away from me.

I raised it. I spoke louder. I began to think of how evangelists talk, throwing their voices into the rear of stadiums. I tried it. It worked. My voice flew afar, and I guess my message was being received for I had silence.

Fright suddenly came over me as I heard this silence. I stopped my fright by talking faster. I kept on talking, then suddenly I realized I was pushing too hard and too fast. I slowed up to a better pace.

I went over with the people.

This was a great moment in my speaking life. I had met success by selling confidence to my audience, confidence I had something that would help them make sales, and that "Sales Mean Jobs."

I was helping people get jobs. It was a great feeling. I believe my audience felt my thrill, and that is perhaps how I won their confidence. I let them feel I was sincerely and honestly trying to be of help.

I believe it was Lincoln who said that if you are to win a man to your cause you must convince him that you are a friend.

If you will do this in front of an audience, you'll have them on your side. You can then help that audience raise their sights to whatever you want them to see, providing they feel your sincerity.

Read Benjamin Franklin and note how he lists enthusiasm as one of the greatest of all ways to excite people to your way of thinking, to win them over to your cause.

Audiences buy enthusiastic speakers. Great messages delivered with a blank stare and a courtroom delivery never go across with audiences. Better a weak message greatly given than a great one given poorly.

I learned another great lesson in walking onto a homemade platform in the center of the Cotton Bowl, Dallas, Texas, to face twenty thousand people, and that is: *Don't fear failure.*

Respect failure, because it hardens you, and teaches you things that success cannot teach you.

It is often said that the best time to prepare a speech is right after you have given one, when the triumphs and failures of your last speech are fresh in your mind.

Have a curb conference with yourself after each speech. A curb conference in selling is when the salesman and his trainer sit on a curb, after having made a sale or failed to make one, and discuss what was good and what was bad in the presentation inside the lady's house.

Have a curb conference with yourself. Ask: Did I catch their attention in my first ten words? Did I keep up interest? Did I close with a demand?

Analyze your talk from stem to stern, and at once improve it or write another talk while this one is still fresh on your mind.

You learn how to hammer nails by practice. You learn how to play a piano by practice. That is the only way to learn how to meet people, win them over, and banish fear. Practice meeting people.

Meet people often. Go up to the butcher, the banker, the streetcar conductor. Ask him a simple question to practice meeting and talking with people without having a fear of them.

Then visit a neighbor. Talk with him. Talk with a group of them. Then join a small club of some sort, and hobnob with others. Be a good listener first, a good talker second.

Once you have learned the art of listening, you will have the courage to say things yourself and enjoy the thrill of facing people and enjoying them.

You are a part of everybody you meet, and a part of everything you hear. The more you hear and the more people you meet, the better speaker you will be.

Then when you face twenty or twenty thousand people, the audience will detect your honesty and sincerity, you will win their confidence, and in winning their confidence you will win them.

27

What to Do When Your Talk Fails

I learned this trick from the air pilots. It's the one and only thing to do when you bust up on the platform, or crack up in the living room.

Quite a number of years ago C. R. Smith of American Airlines hired our staff to improve public relations between stewardesses, ticket agents, the sales staff and the public at large.

One of the interesting experiments we made was to have the airlines remove the SAFETY BELTS sign and substitute the less formidable SEAT BELTS.

Remember how in the old days you would see a sign flash on a plane almost shouting at you, HOOK UP YOUR SAFETY BELT! Buzzers would ring, gongs would sound, and stewardesses would run up and down the aisle warning you to fasten your safety belt because there was a big storm ahead.

Some public relations! It scared the life out of the passengers.

Now the airlines say simply: "Please fasten your seat belt."

That is the value of choosing words to influence others. But when you fail, as we all do at times, what should be done?

Go right back and give another speech.

Don't sit back and get more scared, but leap at the first chance to stand up and speak again, this time trying to correct your mistakes.

The pilot knows when he cracks up that the best thing is to get right back into another plane before he has time for "shock" to set in.

That is my advice to you. Give another talk before you have a "speech hangover."

Find another audience before you get too scared ever to want to attempt another speech, or to tell another story before friends. If something has happened at a gathering, go right back and prove it was an accident or that it taught you a lesson and that it won't happen again.

Tell that funny story until they start laughing at what you say, and not at you. Practice makes perfect.

You can't always win. The proper words, the proper delivery, the proper story will help, but there are times when everything fails you.

Then you flop—and I say then is the time to find another group to tell your funny story to, or another platform to give that speech from. Don't let "shock" set in.

Tell the story again, and immediately!

When the customer was told the story about the pretty new headlight on the Hoover and she failed to buy, an alert salesman went back and changed his story and said, "This light sees hidden dirt, madam. Push it under a chair, pull it out—and dirt is gone."

When the red signal was put on the cleaner to tell the operator when it was filled with dirt, many women got scared of the speech given by the salesman to sell them this idea. Women would say, "Must I have a danger signal to warn me it is chewing my rugs?"

With defeat facing him, the alert salesman would tell the woman: "See this red signal? You may forget to clean the bag, but the bag won't forget to remind you!"

His change of pace, his change of idea, his change of words put him over the second time. Good thing he didn't go into shock and say, "I'll never try to sell again!"

So when they have laughed at you instead of your story, curb yourself. Correct the situation. Return—and at once repeat the story with the improvements in it.

28

One Way to Make
People Like You Instantly

The sincere compliment wins more victories for you than any single thing I know.

The compliment, so seldom given, wins you friends.

The compliment turns enemies into friends, turns the casual acquaintance into a bosom companion on a trip.

The compliment is the greatest single way I know to win over an audience.

Stand up, compliment them on their behavior, their looks, their numbers, their city, their climate or their town! Watch them like you instantly!

When I found the Art of the Sincere Compliment, I found a new road to success.

Be sincere and say, "This is my fourth time in your city, and it is still a lovely town to me!"

Or the subtle compliment: "I appreciate sincerely being

invited back here for the fifteenth time to speak to your club." I don't mind telling you this was my approach at the New York Sales Executives Club recently, on my fifteenth visit there.

What greater compliment can you give a club than to thank them for inviting you back? Especially the fifteenth time.

It puts the audience on your side in all of ten seconds!

The compliment makes friends of waiters too, and this any traveler wants to do in self-preservation. I have found it advisable, early in the meal, to compliment the waiter or the restaurant on something, if only to say, "That was certainly fine onion soup."

You so inflate the waiter he makes darned sure the rest of the meal is properly served.

I find it good for my soul when I leave a restaurant to tell the waiter or owner, "I liked that meal. That roast was unusually well cooked." It protects my retreat.

Always try to find something in particular to say. Thanking them for a fine meal is one thing, but to highlight something in particular highlights you in their eyes.

I find the compliment left behind in ticket offices, hotel lobbies, taxicabs, makes me friends as I leave the door.

That is important to my feelings. I don't want to feel a strong stare when I exit from a business office or a public place because I failed to say "Thank you."

I like to tell bellboys, "This look like a fine room." I like to tell porters when I check out, "That was a comfortable room." I like to make them feel proud of their jobs and their employment, for they make me feel good in return.

I would say, therefore, if you want to go far through life as a speaker or just a plain old traveler, learn the Art of the Compliment.

Learn how to compliment, not flatter.

Learn how to make the chairman feel good by saying, "Thank you for a very nice introduction, and now I'd like to tell you my experiences . . ."

Learn how to thank the secretary who hired you. He is your best bet for future dates. Tell him he had a fine meeting. Be specific, too.

When the compliment isn't required, it's a real compliment. When it is sincere, it registers twice as hard.

Compliment, and go far in life.

Compliment the secretary, the boss, the employees. Pass compliments wherever you go, and watch people begin to like you better and say finer things about you.

Don't overlook the family. Compliment them. The dinner will be better.

Compliment the storekeeper on the groceries he gave you last time, and watch him be on the lookout for you the next time.

If you want good steaks, compliment the butcher!

Leave compliments all around you; just be sure they are sincere and not blunt flatteries.

Compliment someone on his hat, his suit, her dress; on the way he told a funny story, on the way he smiles, talks, walks, or on the fact he is just plain happy and friendly all of the time.

The sincere compliment never lets you down.

The potatoes may have been cold, the drinks weak, the coffee too black—but something must have been good enough to compliment.

Find that something, and you'll find success.

29

Getting Along With People

I found that, after all, everybody is a salesman.

The doctor, the lawyer, the undertaker, the schoolmarm, the detective, the receptionist at the entrance, all are salespeople.

All must have something to sell, something to get across to the other person, if only their personalities, their smiles, or the fact they are good to have around.

The more you know about selling, the better you are in whatever job you have, for selling is speaking—and speaking is selling.

Learn the one art and you automatically begin to learn something of the other art.

Selling, you see, goes hand in hand with speaking. Knowing what to say and how to say it makes you a better conversationalist. Here's a simple formula to help you get yourself across with others:

THE FIVE WHEELERPOINTS

1. *Don't Sell the Steak—Sell the Sizzle.* It's the sizzle that sells the steak, and not the cow. The sizzle appeals to the heart, the steak to the brain.
2. *Don't Write—Telegraph.* Your first ten words are more important than your next ten thousand. Watch your first ten words and they'll always watch out for you.
3. *Say It With Flowers.* It's as much what you *do* as what you *say* that makes people react. Never say anything without doing something to prove the point.
4. *Don't Ask If—Ask Which.* Always give others a choice between *something* and *something,* never between *something* and *nothing.*
5. *Watch Your Bark.* It's *how* you say *what* you say, so watch the tone of your voice.

The New Sixth Wheelerpoint

6. *Proper Timing.* Knowing *when* to say or to do it is as important as knowing what to say and do.*

Talking before Rotarians, Kiwanis, Lions, Optimists, standing up and saying a few words to a Jaycee meeting or

---

* These Wheelerpoints are from Elmer Wheeler's books, *Tested Sentences That Sell, Sizzlemanship, How to Make Your Sales Sizzle in 17 Days, Selling Dangerously, Tested Ways to Close the Sale.*

a P.T.A. group is one thing—but to hold the attention of a group of salesmen is another thing.

Salesmen are versatile. I can remember when I sold the evening edition of the Baltimore *News,* my sales sizzle was, "The evening hours are the reading hours." I tried to show my customers that here was the time to relax and really make a note of what might be purchased next day.

When I did a stretch one summer advising a morning newspaper on its sales sizzles, I found that the opposite appeal was good too, having the sales staff say, "The morning paper catches the reader on the way downtown while the ads are still fresh on his mind."

You see there are two sides to everything. Tolerance is to hear both sides and then make your decision. To be dogmatic in front of people and claim yours is the only way is a big mistake. It is better to say, tolerantly, of the other person: "I can see where Jim Jones feels the evening hours are the reading hours. He has something there. I believe, though, that reading an ad at breakfast keeps it fresher on the reader's mind, don't you?"

Tolerance. Give and take. These are qualities for anyone to assume. Use the "Yes, but—" technique in selling yourself to others. Say: "Yes, I can see the point of my opponent. The defense has a good idea there, but—" and away you go on your point.

The same rule applies at sales meetings, with noise, disinterested people and loud talking. You must fight through

146

these disturbances and not let them bother you. Be tolerant with the audience.

Learn to roll with the blows. Don't dare to criticize them. Don't dare to show annoyance. They'll fight you all the harder.

Be patient with trouble. Join it. You can't whip a group of any size no matter how you shout if mentally they are asleep, or if they prefer to be noisy rather than listen.

In our training schools we have one session called the "Normal disturbance session," wherein a speaker must keep right on talking while members of the audience drink water, stand up, move around, pass notes to the chairman, raise and lower windows, write on the blackboard, open and close doors —normal disturbances you'll find in any meeting.

Another sesson is called the "Snoring Session," wherein the speaker finds his audience all leaning on their elbows, as if in great interest as he starts to speak. If he is good they lean farther forward, but if he is pretty bad they lean backward and start snoring.

The worse the speaker, the greater the snores.

This is mighty good training in patience and tolerance— how to stand up, say something simple, win attention, ask for action, and close the speech.

I have been taught a lot on tolerance by long-winded story-tellers who corner you and proceed to tell you a twenty-minute yarn about an ant that you have already heard twice that day.

I have learned not to encourage the peripatetic table-hopper, argue with a gentleman, or forget to light a lonesome wife's cigarette.

I have learned to be patient with the fellow who tells and retells the same old experience he had on a train, a bus or "last night down at the bar." He tells it once. Tells it twice. Then begins all over.

You must be tolerant—and have patience.

I believe these two things will get you farther along your road to triumph out in public than any other qualities I can name. Be tolerant with others. Be patient with their weaknesses.

You will come out a winner if you learn the art of side-stepping trouble with a smile. Many a pugilistic conventioner who wants to fight anybody and everybody can be calmed down by a smile.

The smile, the soft word, will turn away anger.

It is a great art, that of getting along with people, and two of the greatest sales strategies I know are:

Be tolerant with others.

Be patient with their weaknesses.

30

Trade Secrets for Speakers

I never realized some 6,110 speeches ago the value of over-coming fear by one rule: Cultivate a little *"I don't give a damn"* spirit.

It will put you over, for it will banish fear of meeting people faster than anything I know.

I have found, you see, in speaking to people by the thousands, that an audience loves a good loser.

It is an old axiom that *people will forget your failures the minute you become a success.*

I learned, too, the value of enthusiasm, the one thing most bosses will buy faster than anything else; for they feel they can always train the enthusiastic person, but have no chance with one who lacks this secret ingredient of successful people.

Enthusiasm can't be purchased. Know-how can be purchased—but it is of no value if you are one who can't get yourself and your ideas across to others in an enthusiastic manner.

I would say that if you will keep enthusiasm long enough, you will gain whatever goal in life you have daydreamed about.

I had always believed you must talk for a couple of hours to sell an idea to an audience, until I realized that after forty-five minutes no one is listening anyway. If he is, he is so filled with ideas he won't get what else is being said.

After forty-five minutes (often thirty) you can't sell yourself, or an idea, to anyone at a mass meeting of people.

I believe it took Abraham Lincoln only two minutes to give his famous speech at Gettysburg.

Why, I say then, should you make a speech long? It isn't the length that counts, but the ideas and thoughts packed in it that put you over with others. The quickie funny story gets a bigger laugh than the ten-minute long-drawn-out yarn.

Follow this rule: When you have stopped having something to say, it is best to sit down.

I know of no business that hasn't rules, formulas, trade secrets and tricks of the trade. I was glad I was a nosy newspaperman, for I always kept on the lookout for them.

So that when I was told to "look at the bridge of the listener's nose, not stare him in the eyes," I marked down that rule and used it.

How it helps me in tight places, where there is a lot of tension! I find that if I look away from my man, he feels I am jittery, scared or not sure of my story. If I look him squarely in the eye, there is a lot of embarrassment, and I forget my sales presentation.

But when you look at the bridge of his nose or at his mouth, then there isn't the stare of two pairs of eyes looking at each other, and the speaker and the listener both are more relaxed.

I learned another rule. If distractions annoy you, then practice giving your speech in front of a TV set, or a radio or a phonograph that is turned on. Talk and keep on talking and practice not letting what you hear bother you. This is excellent training for the speaker who occasionally speaks before a sales meeting or club and finds noise a distraction.

Life is sweet and easy to one who will look for the rules, then follow them. I tried to find footsteps of others ahead of me so that I could go down the trail of life and not lose out too often. When I found such steps, I welcomed them.

I learned in Mexico never to have "one last drink" with friends. You know the old expression of a North American, "one for the road." In Mexico they never have a "last" drink.

"Last is such a sad word," said my friend Federico Sanchez F., "and we never like to hear it."

He then raised his glass and said, *"Penultimo!"*

That means, as you can readily guess, "next to the last." I like that idea in closing this story of my lifetime experiences and adventures in going from a tongue-tied reporter to a

151

speaker. That there is no "last" to anything.

Even this book: for I hope to be here 7,110 speeches from now, and I trust no one will ever feel this is the "last" speech when Elmer comes to town.

I want to think that the chairman, when he signs me off, will hold up a glass of whatever it is in front of him and say one Mexican word to me: *"Penultimo!"*

3 TESTED FRIEND-FIZZLERS

1. "In other words!" Say it right the first time, and you won't have to put it "in other words." Conserve your energy—and the other person's nerves.

2. "What I meant to say was . . ." You are actually saying that you didn't know what you were saying the first time. Don't repeat yourself.

3. "To make myself clearer!" Brother, you mean that you think the other fellow is pretty dumb . . . so you will make it clearer for the poor sap!

CLICHÉS

If you really want to *annoy* people and *lose friends* try some of these nerve-testers:

"See what I mean?"
"Get it . . .?"
"Catch on?"
"Ya understand?"
"Natch . . .!"
"See . . .?"

The *Big Secret* in annoying others effectively is to tag these "clichés" onto every other sentence you say—*"See?"*

"To make myself clearer," anything you repeat over and over annoys people. *"Catch on?"*

153

31

How to Meet Fear
with Brave Thoughts

What is fear? Who has it? What can be done about it?

I have told you how many average people meet fear but here is how a man in one of the most dangerous occupations gained courage.

Manolete was the greatest of all bullfighters. He started the trend of passes that are so colorful in bullfighting. It was Juan Belmonte who created the idea of passes and Manolete who popularized them.

Something has to be done when a two-ton black bull charges down on you. Either you jump back or flag him around you with a cape. Up until Juan Belmonte, bullfighters leaped back away from the bull.

Poor Juan was short-legged and couldn't leap. All he could do was flag the bull around him with his red cape.

Thus he started the present trend in bullfighting, in which the fighter is declared greatest when the bull gets so close to him it rubs blood on his chest.

Manolete made much of Belmonte's methods. He created many original uses of the cape.

What did he do about fear? Manolete said: "To fight a bull when you are not scared is nothing. But to fight a bull when you are scared—that is something."

He would say to the *señoritas,* "Excuse me if I don't talk much, but I am very scared."

Yet when in the ring he would calmly let the horns of the bull graze the gold braid on his costume, his "suit of lights."

Manolete once told the writer Barnaby Conrad, "My knees start to quake when I first see my name on the posters and they don't stop until the end of the season."

Here was a man, much like any other person in public, who admitted to his fear, and in admitting it did away with it. He accepted fear. Each Moment of Truth, that moment when he put the sword into the bull, could be fraught with fear.

At this critical moment, frail man overcomes a one-half-ton Miura bull, as he charges a mile a minute toward the sword. Here, say the experts, is when the real truth inside a man comes out. If there is fear in him, then is when it shows up and the man runs or is killed.

I would say the speaker's Moment of Truth is when he stands up and suddenly faces a two-ton audience.

Here stands the speaker, face to face with an audience as bewildered perhaps as the bull, wondering who this person is that is brave enough to stand up in front of it, with apparently no fear in him.

At this Moment of Truth the speaker says something. If he smiles, if what he says is catching to the audience, a gesture is made to their hearts. He has gotten himself by them for a moment.

The bullfighter uses his cape in veronicas and *pasos de pecho* (chest passes) to keep the bull moving toward him and around him, amusing himself and the audience at the same time.

The speaker uses words to lead his audience to him and around him, with wit, humor and information. He uses passes too, making the audience ready for the kill at the time he reaches his own climax and asks the audience to buy what he came to sell them.

The speaker is indeed a fighter. His ring is the platform, and just as the matador must work his bull around to the right spot in the ring for the kill, so does the speaker have to work the audience into a position to get his point across.

It is well known that a bull has a favorite part of the ring, and that if he is made to leave it, the fighter has an opportunity to win over the beast.

The speaker, like the matador, often plays with his audience with jokes and funny stories, softening up the audience the way the *banderilleros* soften up the bull with their spiked sticks.

156

The speaker must find out too, in a hurry, which way his audience is inclined to move, so he can move with them, or change their direction and so win them over.

The matador has no more than fifteen minutes, on the average, to meet the bull and kill him. For inside of fifteen minutes a bull suddenly learns about Man and what he is doing, and if the bull lasts over fifteen minutes his chances of killing the Man are good—for he learned about Man in fifteen minutes.

Up until he first faced the matador, the bull was never among men very much. They were strangers to him. Once, as a young bull, he was tested for his brave heart; but if he passed this test, never again was he among men or horses much until he suddenly charged into the bull ring.

Yet, inside of fifteen minutes, he so analyzes Man that he can kill him. That is why the matador must act swiftly or be killed. Why he must quickly decide whether the bull hooks to the left or to the right.

The speaker has fifteen minutes himself before an audience starts really to judge him. If he passes this test by clever weaving of his cape of stories, then he will last the other fifteen minutes assigned to an average noonday speaker, or another thirty or forty minutes if he is an evening speaker.

The matador conquers fear back in that little church room he prays in just before coming into the ring. Once he is in the ring he has no fear. The bull can't smell fear because fear was conquered before the matador came into the ring.

A speaker must conquer his fear too. He must do so before he stands up, for an audience can "smell fear" just as a bull can smell fear, get angry and kill the frightened matador whose judgment is clouded up with anxiety, worry, tension.

Leave tension off the platform. It can tighten up your facial gestures, your throat, your words! It can tighten up an audience with a tension that no cape movements will ever release.

Manolete used to say, "They keep demanding more and more of me every day." How true that is of a speaker. Each time they demand more. You must keep moving forward each time, giving something new and different and holding the attention of your audience to earn their bravos.

You are only as good as your last speech. If the speech was good, you are still good. If not you aren't good. You must win each audience each time, as the matador must kill the bull each time or be hissed and booed out of popularity.

Like the bullfighter, you must learn which way the audience moves, which way it sways, so you won't be fooled into acting wrongly. One error won't mean death to you, as to a Manolete. To you it may mean momentary loss of a laugh, loss of a moment of friendliness, but you can always pull out of it.

Manolete was allowed only one miss. Which is why he had fear. Why he overcame it by swift analysis of the bull to ascertain its habits, which way it raised or lowered its killing horns.

I am told that confusion kills more bullfighters than any other one thing. The confusion that comes when fear suddenly overtakes him and he loses control of his audience and it gets away from him.

How to avoid fear? *Get so absorbed in what you are doing there is not time for fear or worry.*

The bull is charging Manolete. He can't afford fear. He gets absorbed in his veronica to lead the bull around him, or he decides to let the sword go into the lowered neck of the bull, since only when the neck is lowered can a kill be made.

What keeps him so absorbed? It is knowledge. Knowledge of what bulls do, how they react, how they charge. Manolete has facts.

For facts rob you of fear. Facts tell you there is no fear to fear. Facts show you the way and you can then become so absorbed that, as with Manolete, you have no time for fear.

Keep your mind busy. Keep it so busy there is no room for fear to enter. Lose yourself in action, as did Manolete, for in holding the attention of a bull or an audience, you forget fear and it leaves you.

That seems the way to relieve yourself of tension in a roomful of strangers; before either a charging bull or a charging audience.

George Bernard Shaw said, "The secret of being miserable is to have leisure to be miserable."

Put it this way. If Manolete gave himself leisure to fear

death, he'd go into the ring with tensions. He'd lose his deft footwork, his skilled muleta or capework. He would be killed.

If you allow yourself time to get scared, you'll find fear will go with you right onto the platform. So banish fear before the door opens at the gay gathering and you are to meet strangers that scare the life out of you; leave fear at the speaker's table, and keep it from the microphone and the audience.

32

6-Point Formula to Success

For the past ten years I have been writing a newspaper column called "Success Secrets" based on interviews with people who have become famous. I ask them what advice, suggestions or magic formulas they have to offer the world as the secrets of their success.

So far I have written up some thousand men and women, most of whom became millionaires financially as well as in health and happiness.

One day I decided to examine all the advice, rules and formulas these people told me they used to become successful, to see if I couldn't find a pattern that anyone could use.

Believe it or not I found that pattern—a formula that you can use to become a success in talking with people.

I found that each of my thousand millionaires, most of whom were successes in meeting people and in conversation, and often on the platform, had become a success through the similarity of six things each did either consciously or subconsciously—but mostly consciously.

Each had the same formula, in round figures, and each put it to about the same dramatic use in his own rise from unknown to known, from poor boy to rich boy. Each followed about the same identical path.

I will give this formula to you now and I hope it will help you as it has these one thousand other normal, regular people go up the ladder to gain their daydreams, to see their own castles in Spain become real brick and mortar.

Six Tested Steps to Your Success!

Step 1: Know what you want

If you don't know what you want, how can you gain it? So say to yourself, "I want a million"—"I want a mink coat"—"I want people to listen to me." Know what you want in life, then you will have a chance to get it. Each of my thousand millionaires knew what he wanted.

Step 2: Put it on paper

Get it out of your brain, onto paper. Blueprint your castle in Spain. Put it in front of you where you can see it morning, noon and night. It will then work on another emotion, the emotion of sight. Remember, the Empire State Building was once a dream on paper. Conrad Hilton, owner of the Waldorf, always carried a picture of the hotel wherever he went and looked at it constantly.

Step 3: Know where to start

If you want to be an oil millionaire, go to Texas. If you want to be a dress designer, go to the dress capitals of the world. If you want to speak, be among people. Knowing where to start your daydream on to success is important.

Step 4: Set it in motion

Too many daydreams sit idly by, waiting for someone to start them off. There are thousands of inventions in the patent offices waiting for someone to work them. It took an apple vendor to get me in action. What will start you off? What will set you in motion?

Step 5: Don't settle for less

If your dream is to own a mink, don't settle for muskrat. For once you get your daydream in motion, it requires only a slight push on the hoop to keep up the momentum. Never settle for less than your daydreams. None of my thousand millionaires settled for less than they dreamed about.

Step 6: Know when to relax

Once you've gained your goal, do as these thousand people have done and relax and enjoy it. Remember you are today what you daydreamed about yourself ten years ago. Don't stop going forward, but don't crowd your success. Don't be overly greedy. Sit back and enjoy life. You'll be happier.

163

33

The Joys and Trials of
a Speaker's Life

Life as a speaker isn't only beer and skittles; it is often champagne on the one hand and 6 A.M. trips to a plane on the other.

However, the joy of traveling and meeting people is one that has so many pleasures and fun for me that the troubles are soon forgotten.

I helped my travel life considerably one day when I decided to send out in advance some forty-four ways on "How to Care for and Feed the Speaker," which you will find in detail at the end of this life's story.

This little leaflet kept me from getting too many unpleasant rooms, some even with the fire escape through my room. It kept the gravy from stacking up in front of a talkative vice-president at a banquet, and it got me my

164

fees after my talk instead of six months later.

Indeed, there is fun for a speaker.

As I look back at all the fun awards and fun stunts pulled on me (usually to sell more tickets for my talk), I believe that sitting in the jail at San Antonio before my talk that night at the Sales Executives Club was a genuinely amusing highlight.

Perhaps another was the time the Fort Worth Club had a parade and put me on a wooden horse and had me towed through the streets, because "Elmer is an Easterner from Dallas."

I got even with them, though, when I invented my Sizzle Ranch slogan, "Where the East Peters Out," because Fort Worth's city slogan was, "Where the West Begins." Then, too, the publicity sold ten thousand tickets and Amon Carter turned out to introduce me and gave me one of the Texas hats he was famous for giving people.

I believe one of the finest and rarest honors given me was when the Dallas Sales Club made me an Honorary Texas Ranger, and gave me a bronze plaque to put on the rear of my car. It sure helps at certain times when an overly industrious traffic officer starts crowding me.

I think the most amusing and unusual award was being made an Honorary Ozark Hillbilly by the Springfield, Missouri, Chamber of Commerce.

On the other hand, I can recall being grounded by planes for hours, although I am always cautious about too close a schedule. Many speakers make a big error in arriving by plane a few hours ahead of their talk. Often they don't arrive.

It is always well to protect yourself in some way, so that if a plane is grounded you have other means of arriving for your speaking date. Don't worry the committee!

I have always said that what I get paid for is the travel and sitting around before and after the talk, especially in airports. Here is where you really earn your money.

I have more fun at my talks than the audience, but less fun once I am en route.

I have learned never to count on the early rousers getting me to the planes. It is always safer to let the cab company participate in my departure.

Since so much of the life of a speaker is passed in hotel bedrooms, I always try to get the best. The best ones, unfortunately, are always on the second floor front, overlooking the cab stands or the bus or streetcars.

I'd prefer a quiet back room. They are usually half the price too, and that is something in the life of many a speaker. But hotels like to give "the best" to the speaker. This is another way of saying, "Give him the works!"

Then there are the committeemen who keep coming to your room, and think nothing of running up a big telephone bill on you, ordering things from the hotel or otherwise adding to the speaker's bill. "We pay him amply, don't we?" seems to be their philosophy.

Of late years I have been able to scotch this attitude by

making "plus hotel room" part of my deals, and now I don't care who comes up or what girl friend they want to call in Japan.

One of the delights in going to a hotel is to have alert managers send you the basket of fruit, the bottle of drink, or the usual "hotel gift" they reserve for speakers to make them good publicity agents for their hotels.

One outstanding event in my life occurred when the Chattanooga Sales Club put a card under the fruit which read, "This entitles you to telephone your wife while you are our guest."

That night, just as I was appearing on the platform, Mrs. Wheeler received a bouquet of roses, "Because we know you miss your husband and we have him tonight."

It is little thoughts like this that make life as a speaker worth while.

The speaker is always subject to a lot of drinking before his talk, and the unwise speakers join in the festivities, some too well. A cocktail party that lasts over thirty minutes is dangerous to both speaker and audience.

I find that the boys, out for the night with Elmer, are always inclined to try to make a Russian soldier of him, and seem hurt if he doesn't fall on the floor. Foolishly, they think this is a sign of being a great guy.

It is always dangerous, too, for the speaker, after his regular talk, to get into a bull session with a lot of off-color stories with wives present.

Someone always tries to start the speaker off on these

stories, and they aren't received favorably by all.

I have learned there are certain amusing yarns that will go over in an after-speech group and not let you down with the nondrinking, nonstory-listening part of the gathering. These are not quite suitable for the platform, yet are not the so-called "dirty" stories.

I try to avoid late hours. The present night's committee can sleep the next night but Poor Elmer must be met by a fresh audience the next night, and can't show up with last night's bags under his eyes. Getting away from an all-night "performance" is perhaps the hardest thing for a speaker to do and still maintain his good-fellowship standing.

I have another phobia in common with most speakers, that is, visiting the local courthouse. I have seen them all. Yet most committees seem compelled to brag about their courthouses (or some other local spot), and the speaker must go there and rave about the sight.

Certain other sights I do enjoy, such as homes, new projects, or some local historical spot. These are interesting— but not the courthouse!

I always fear, too, being asked to stay overnight with the president in his home. I'd much prefer a hotel, where I can receive my friends and telephone calls, and brush my teeth at will.

Most speakers enjoy this hotel privacy.

I always worry, too, about an overly energetic committee that wants to stick right with you up to the speech, then hang on until the wee hours. Most speakers like to rest in the late afternoon and often catch a few cat winks before the talk.

I find that eating after an early talk is best. Feeding and wining a speaker before a talk, then shoving him onto the platform and saying, "Go to it," is like feeding a horse before a race.

I find also, that one big problem of a speaker is proper dress. Usually the local head table likes to dress all in dark, usually blue, and when the speaker dresses that way he is in a "uniform."

I like always to wear a conservative suit, but not the typical "dark blue" banquet uniform. A bigger problem is what to wear so that you can speak in both the South and the North in the same week and stay in keeping with the weight of a suit. I find the answer is a very light summer-winter-weight suit, but of such a character that it can be worn in the cold North and not look summery.

I find that lightweight suits are best since platforms do get mighty steamed up under the smoke and lights and heat.

Giving the talk, if you really enjoy talking and meeting people, is the easy part of the speaker's life. One big headache for most speakers is the banquet.

Ah, the banquet! Having to sit next to the gabby wife of the vice-president. Every time you try to eat a forkful of chicken (tightly fastened to the bone), she asks you a question such as, "How'd you get in the speaking business, anyway?"

This can easily take two hours to answer, unless you sum

it all up by saying, "Oh, I just like to talk."

Then come the other questions such as, "How long have you been married?"—"Any children?"—"Does Mrs. W. travel with you?"—"I don't suppose you are ever home?"—"How many miles do you travel a year?"—"It must be fun traveling, isn't it?"—"Ever meet Katy Jones in Dallas?"

Then about that time around comes the three-piece string orchestra or some cowboy with a "stomach Steinway," and plays your state song so long and loud it rings forever in your ears and you can't talk for an hour.

How I love the state songs! Round and round goes the gal or fellow with the "belly organ," playing state songs until you hear all forty nine of them—or else. Yes, or else some drunk stands up and shouts, "Shay, what's wrong with Rhode Island, huh?"

Always at banquets, dinners, luncheons, there is the drunk away from home. The guy who "you know, back home he is the soberest guy in town, but when he gets away from his wife, look out for him."

Then there is the "wolf away from home," always looking for the pretty gals. Always has one he introduces as his "niece."

Or the singer. The guy back home who is quiet as a mouse, but put two jiggers in him, and he thinks he can sing "Where the River Shannon Flows," and because he has a few friends egging him on, he really believes he has a voice.

Then, of course, there are the flock of hand-shakers at the

170

speaker's table, all wanting to be seen shaking your hand, just about the time you are ready to raise one of those over-hard rolls or a scoop of melted ice cream. Out comes a big paw and a voice that says, "Bet you don't know me, do you?" What's a fellow to reply to that one?

But it's fun. You enjoy life. You meet many people. You sit in fancy suites, get the finest service your own wife back home would never think of giving you; you get flattery from the gals and scotch and sodas on the house from the men.

Well, on the whole, speaking is fun and I believe I'd choose it again as a career if it were offered me, or as a hobby, a side line or a way to sell myself, my services or my product to others.

Because it is great talking to people. Fun being in many different places. Profitable, too.

It is a thrill to walk into a roomful of friends and realize you are welcome as an interesting person to know, one with a gift for carrying on a conversation without being a bore. One who can tell a story that gets laughs and the comment, "He's sure a great storyteller, isn't he?"

It raises the ego. It flatters the soul. It stimulates the the body. I like being a speaker.

I like being a speaker because it gives you the greatest education in the world, one you can't get out of schools or books.

I like being a speaker because you get the greatest ex-periences in the world, and plenty of adventures too.

It is a thrill walking into a hotel lobby, an airport or a convention auditorium, and have people come up and shake your hand and tell you they heard you once and want to hear you again.

I like being a speaker, too, for the help you give people. When someone comes out of an audience and says, "I had a small job, but you taught me how to sell. Now I am sales manager of my firm," what a satisfaction that gives you.

It fills your soul and heart and mind with a spirit of good fellowship, as you sit back and realize you have done some good in this world.

I am glad, therefore, that an apple in the streets of Baltimore stirred me into action, and showed me the way to triumph over my early fear of meeting people and speaking to them.

I'd do it all over again!

34

What It Takes to Be
a Paid Public Speaker

I have often been asked, do people vary in their reactions to speakers in various parts of the country? That is, will the same story or joke go over with equal response in New York, Des Moines and Los Angeles?

I have found that it will.

There are exceptions, of course, but people usually all laugh at about the same things in fifty million homes when a national TV comedian is on the air.

The exceptions are due perhaps to local situations. You can't make fun of rain in a dry area where the farmers are suffering; and you can't talk about integration in the Southern cities troubled with this problem. The big-city listener may not react as well as you might expect from a speech on "How to Raise Onions," and the midwestern dental society may not react too much to a story on "Life in Boston."

But if you plan your jokes, your stories, your conversation, your lecture to fit the locale, then the same reaction will come at the same time in similar situations.

The French in Montreal are a fine audience. They are very emotional and react in a hurry to any action you give them. They will giggle, laugh, applaud if you arouse them. They like lots of action, arm movements and facial gestures.

They all expect you to talk like their favorite movie actor or star, and I believe Maurice Chevalier is still the big ideal with the French. They like his gestures, his flirtatious mannerisms and his jaunty attitude. Use a little of this and they'll love you in any French-Canadian city.

In New England you must earn your applause. They will sit back on their hands for a while, until you have shown them you are not a phony. They hate phonies in New England, and in true Vermont manner, will give you as much enthusiasm as Cal Coolidge was noted for giving.

Show them how to make money and they'll listen. They will try to figure if you are fooling them; but once you have passed their Blue Nose Test you will have a sincere audience. The Irish, of course, at all times will give you a real run for your money. If you are good, the drinks are on them; if they don't like you, brother, they'll tell you off to your face.

The New Yorker is very erudite. You can't tell him much he hasn't known before, but if you do find something new that hasn't been in the morning edition, the *New Yorker* magazine, or the *Wall Street Journal*, then you will go over with him.

Once you convince him the boy from the sticks has something on the ball, he'll get hep on you and will buy you a double martini, providing you want it ultra-dry, which the New Yorker feels is a great mark of distinction.

The Midwesterner is about that way: midway. He can take you or not. He is less analytical than his Eastern brothers. He'll like you if you don't wear a Madison Avenue suit and a derby. You can't high-hat him, but you can bring him "ideas from the East."

The Southerner is more genteel. He is slow to hate you, slow to accept you. You must slow up your pace a bit in talking with him so he can absorb all you say, and give him time to decide whether you are a friendly Yankee or a Carpetbag leftover trying to hoodwink him.

He isn't as inclined to invite you to his home as the Far Westerner, who will almost yank you into his big car for a drink in the patio or a barbecue. The Southerner is a thinker. He may think longer than others before he applauds, but when he does, you are in and may be invited, in a few years, to visit his home.

You'll go over in the Western states if you don't smack too much of Park Avenue. You can have a little Michigan Boulevard on you, some high polish on the shoes; but don't wear any of the Park Avenue imports from Italy out where the West begins, or you'll peter out.

The wide-open-space boys like just that: wide spaces and wide hats. A derby hat is something they used to shoot at in the old days. They may like their jeans tight, but they sure don't want their lectures filled with tight-fitting ideas. In Sheridan they'll take a stronger drink and a stronger joke than they will in Lima, Ohio.

They will want their steaks rare with hash browns or french fries on the side; while the Southerner will want his corn bread and fried chicken, and expect you to like it with him. He will drink his bourbon, but he is apt to do it quietly in a bar or a home den. The man from Phoenix is apt to stop his car on the dusty road and offer you a snort.

He will perhaps give you lots of pats on the back about what you have said, most of which will be sincere, but he isn't inclined to criticize you. He'd rather let you go away thinking all you said was great, when actually, he didn't approve of half you said.

He just figures it is fine to be friendly with you, pardner. To make you feel welcome. He never says, "Good-bye," but always says, "Hurry back!" He means it too. He wants you to hurry back and talk some nonsense with him. He's friendly.

Now when you go to the Pacific Coast you just divide your reaction in half. From San Francisco south you will be given a great time by all. They will fight duels to see who will meet you at the airport, but they are also inclined to flip a coin next morning to see "who's gonna drive the speaker back to the airport?"

176

You will find "leftovers" from all parts of America in the southern part of the Pacific Coast, and because of that you won't get any true reactions. You may be kidded a lot. You may be patted on the back and given a handout of oranges, but it is well to sit back and enjoy it as you go along. But don't depend on getting to the airport except by established car.

Now once you find a real Californian, then, of course, this doesn't count. He's as generous, as big, as friendly as any home-grown Texan, and you'll be given courtesies, the sincere ones of the conquistadors. But the influx of strangers has watered down the people, and "originals" are hard to find these days in California, and are getting harder to find in certain big cities in Texas.

Go to northern California, then up to Vancouver, B.C., and you will find more "natives." Being natives, they are prouder of their cities, towns and people—and they'll drive one hundred miles to meet the plane and then drive you to the next city. "Aw, what's two hundred miles, son—you don't wanna take an old plane, do you?"

Don't expect this service back East, though. The highways won't permit it, and after all, who has time back East for such things?

If you aren't a phony; if you have a message filled with some light touches and some down-to-earth advice; if you aren't too professorial in your address; people will like you.

You must be content, however, to eat chicken and apple pie nine days in a row; and to have the wife of a president talk a leg off you while you try to get the gravy away from a vice-president down the table.

You must be willing to stay grounded in airports on and off at times, and to be kept awake by a rocky Pullman now and then.

You should be the type that doesn't get indigestion too often, and should have tough feet so you can prance around strange hotel bathrooms and not pick up athlete's foot too easily. You must be sort of a tough guy at heart—and germ-proof.

You can't afford to let waiters upset you or get caught in post-speech arguments on religion, politics or Harry Truman. You must learn to nod and listen, instead of talk and cause arguments.

I have often said I get paid for traveling and for listening to people tell me old jokes, and not for the speech. *The speech is free.* I earn my money when the talk is over and the hostess starts telling me about her petunias, and the host tries to drown me in his favorite drink—and the program chairman tries to keep me up all night as an excuse to stay up himself.

Little do these folks realize that the next day the speaker must arrive at the new airport, must get off the plane with a smile on his face, and not a yawn. That he must be prepared to listen to the committee tell him how to give his speech. "You wouldn't mind, would you, giving our Red Cross, Community Chest, the Rotary Club's Circus, the Boy

Scout Rodeo and the Garden Club a little plug, would you?"

You can often spend five minutes plugging local events that everyone knows you were asked to plug anyway, and that the chairman could have done himself and given you five minutes more time for ideas they won't get after you leave.

Indeed, you must like People—understand People—and accept People, or you won't be a good conversationalist, and certainly not a public speaker.

People are pretty much alike, so find out what goes over with your small group, then with a larger group. Then work into the suburban service club for a date, then the downtown clubs, then the next city, then the next state. Then perhaps find yourself a good booking agent and you are in business.

The speaking field is lucrative. It pays well. You'll make lots of money. Dr. Russell Conwell made four million dollars on his famous talk, "Acres of Diamonds," before he stopped giving it.

You can earn from fifty dollars per talk at some local banquet, to fifteen hundred dollars at a national sales convention of some big firm once you are a star name.

Take anything to start with, even "just for expenses." Get lots of practice for that is what makes you the star. A speech only now and then won't keep the tonsils oiled up. Talk lots, often, if only at the Sunday school picnic.

As an ordinary speaker out of town you can earn $100 to

179

$150 per talk. As you get better, you will find it easy to ask for expenses plus this fee. Then you can go up the scale. The good speaker today gets from $350 to $700 per talk, plus expenses. The star gets $1,000 to $1,500. He must be a national name to get this figure.

As a speaker, you will be asked to give free speeches locally. That is fine. But give a speech other than the one you are paid for, so when it comes to hearing the paid speech, you will get paid for it. Something for nothing is never appreciated even by the local service boys.

Once you have decided to be a "paid speaker" let the world know you are a paid speaker, and that if the doctor will give you a free operation, and the lawyer in the club will draw up a free will, then you'll gladly give a free speech.

One warning: If you are really going in for paid speaking, then be sure your speaking dates are close together. You will waste money if one talk is in Poughkeepsie and the next one in the Panhandle. You will get good fees, but so will the airlines and railroads.

Try to book yourself "tight." Keep yourself occupied each night in a row, and in a given area. Then go home and relax until another series of dates.

Try to avoid cold parts of America during the winter months when travel is not reliable. Book yourself in these spots early in the fall, and late in the spring. Try the South for the winter—but unfortunately, you will never go where you want to go at the time you want. That's why speakers get paid.

180

Miami wants you in August, Calgary in January. The chambers of commerce will sell you on how nice the town is at these off-season times, but believe me, this ain't the case. I love Miami, but in season. I like the Northern clime, but in season.

If you can get to cities in season, you are a lucky speaker.

I have no booking agent. I do the job myself. But until you are recognized, you might want to consider one.

You will need to tell them who you are and the subjects you speak on. Then they will add you to their list of speakers and get out a circular on you.

You will then be booked by the agency exclusively. They won't take you if they don't get all your bookings, or if another booker has you listed.

Until you are known, you may have to pay around 25 to 35 per cent to the booker. He will do all the work booking you, arranging the fees, often your transportation, and will collect the money and send what is due you. You usually accept so much for a talk and pay all of your own expenses. You can refuse to accept any talks you choose.

That is why the booker gets his fee. He does all the work except the travel and giving the speeches and listening to a group of merry housewives gurgle over you after the speech in the den of the wife of the leading citizen.

Your local chamber of commerce secretary can get you started on hiring a booking agent. He, no doubt, has lots of correspondence from many, and you can write them all and see which deal sounds the best for you.

181

It is perhaps advisable at the start to employ a good booking agent and ride along with him for a few seasons. Maybe forever, if you and he work out all right together.

I hope I haven't been too academic in these last few pages, but I figured you might like to learn a little about the inside of speaking and how to go over with people everywhere and earn money in a lucrative field.

One last suggestion: Choose a subject you feel will find the widest audience. No one can help you on this. But we all can advise one thing, that you give a speech with a purpose behind it. Be humorous, if you want. Be witty, like the usual run of preachers and attorneys who "speak for the fun of it." But have a message in your speech.

Fun is fun at the free noonday luncheon, but when people plank down good dollars for a sales-meeting speaker, or a city-wide civic speaker, better leave them with more than the latest jokes or the "funniest stories I ever heard."

35

The Care and Feeding
of Speakers

There is as much of an art to introducing the speaker as to
being a speaker.

Who but a policeman can tell you most about crooks? Who
but a chef knows most about enjoying food?

Who but a speaker can tell you most about what to do in
making a speaker feel happy?

It has been said by Dick Borden and others that all the
audience wants to know about a speaker is:

Why the speaker?

Why the speaker at this time?

Why the speaker at this time before this audience?

If you put this simple rule to use, you won't fail as the
perfect introducer.

I have died a thousand deaths waiting to be introduced.

I have died a thousand more deaths while being introduced.

I have sweated out the chairman's introducing everybody in the audience, to a point where I am about the only one that is left.

I have sat through choral singing and tap dancing. I have heard duets, quartets and people filled up with quarts, trying to entertain while the tables are being cleared.

I have seen chairmen so nervous they can't eat; they even forget your name, let alone why in thunder you are there.

In fact, at times, I think speakers need a good union to provide rules and regulations against boring chairmen, amateur comedians and the town's "big man."

I have seen chairmen fumble so nervously they lost their glasses, dropped their papers, and otherwise made the audience so sorry for them that the poor cusses died a thousand deaths themselves.

However, when a chairman is weak, it doesn't hurt the speaker. It makes audiences feel sorry for him.

That is far better for the speaker than to try winning back an audience after a town comedian has gotten through his routine of a twenty-minute introduction, or given the speaker too big a mountain to climb with his "man who" data.

I die a thousand deaths, too, when the committee puts some gossipy wife of a member next to me.

Just as I am struggling to tear off a piece of white meat,

hoping it doesn't land in my lap, some gal next to me asks, "How did you get to be a speaker?"

Or, just as I am hoping she will pass the gravy stuck in front of her, she asks me, "Do you ever bring your wife on these trips? How many children do you have? Where did you speak last? Where do you go from here?"

I have said it many times. I'll repeat it. You, as the speaker, are a hero upon arrival, and up until the talk is over. Then you become a burden.

They fight duels to see who will meet you at the airports with the news photographers.

They fight to see who will be with you at noon—who will sit next to you at the banquet table that night.

Then the talk is over. The reporters have gone home—and most of your hosts. They get tired too. You are dumped in a hotel lobby or left with a few of the group's late drinkers.

Come morning. All the fellows who said they'd be on hand to ride you to the airport have disappeared. You are left on your own.

Handling the speaker, as you will soon see, is quite an art —and once you learn it you will have many good-will ambassadors, speakers who love you because you knew how to feed and care for them.

There is the introducer who merely says, "He needs no introduction," and sits down, and everybody wonders who you are.

On the other hand, I have seen the town's leading talker

get up and tell fifteen jokes, then fumble for your name as he weakly says, "Here he is."

You can overdo the introduction to a point where the audience soon folds its arms and says, "That speaker better be good with such a build-up." No audience expects more than an ordinary speaker with a nice talk. When the build-up is too great, the speaker has three strikes against him.

Lastly, in this tirade on chairmen, let me say that perhaps the most unnerving of all chairmen is the one who, when you finish your speech stands up and says: "Thank you, Elmer Wheeler. Now next week, folks, we've got a real good speaker coming. Be sure not to miss him."

Here, from the pages of *Future* magazine of the National Junior Chamber of Commerce, are forty-four rules I wrote on "The Care and Feeding of Speakers." These should be of help to you when next you are called on to act as program chairman.

Once upon a time a speaker went to a small town. Because hotels were few and food bad, the wife of the president of the speaking club fed the speaker his supper.

This night she served thick soup, to which the long-haired speaker remarked, "If I ate that heavy soup, I could not give a *good* speech."

When the meat and potatoes arrived, hot and home-cooked, he said, "Oh, my, that would fill me up and I would never give a *good* speech."

On seeing a generous slice of apple pie and ice cream, he

gasped and almost shouted, "Dessert—? It would stuff me so I could never, NEVER give a *good* speech."

Her prized dinner ruined, the wife went to bed with the nervous fidgets or something speakers can bring on; and hubby and the empty speaker went to the town hall for the speech.

When hubby returned, the wife stuck her head from under the quilts long enough to ask, "Did he give a *good* speech?"

"He shoulda et! !" snapped back hubby, and went to bed himself.

Whose fault was this? The speaker or the speaking committee?

Maybe both, but for once, let us give rules for handling and feeding speakers, instead of rules for the speaker to win over his audience.

Your speaker can be the best *national* public-relations booster for your club or city; or the worst, depending upon how you treat him and feed him, and here are some suggestions based on 3,981 speeches during the past nineteen years.

Rule 1. When you first contact the speaker tell him how many people he will address, and whether or not you plan to make a charge to raise money. Speakers charge more when you charge for them, and their fee is based, in part, on size of audience.

Rule 2. Tell speakers the time of your meeting; and if possible, give them a choice of dates. Perhaps they can tie you in with near-by talks, and save you travel costs.

Rule 3. When you agree on fee be sure you understand, together, who will pay transportation, hotel room and restaurant costs.

Rule 4. In your first letter, explain to the prospective speaker how he can arrive in your city; how he can leave. When speakers see it is easy to arrive and leave, by convenient transportation, they are more apt to accept your engagement.

Rule 5. If you are in a country foreign to the speaker, be sure to quote fees in his currency, not yours, to avoid any misunderstanding later on as to exchange.

Rule 6. Meet the speaker on arrival so he won't worry whether or not he arrived on the right day, in the right town.

Rule 7. Take him to his hotel and phone ahead to be sure his room is ready and register him in. Make him glad he came to your city. Don't keep him tired and dirty in a lobby for an hour while some slow maid fixes up a room for him.

Rule 8. Make him feel he is welcome. Go to the room with him, to make sure he didn't get one opposite the public bath, or across from an elevator. Better yet, invest in a suite for him. He'll give you a lot of publicity nationally.

Rule 9. Once settled in his room, let the fellow alone for an hour or so to clean up and put on the dog. Besides, after all night on a Pullman he may have urgent need for the bath!

Rule 10. Tell the speaker your plans for his visit. Have

plans. Don't say, "If you want anything or to do anything, let us know." He won't. Have somebody take him to lunch and dinner; around the town, but spare him the city hall. He's seen too many. Find his interests. Keep him entertained if you expect a good speech that night.

Rule 11. Don't surprise the speaker by all appearing in 1929 Tuxedos. If they are in order, advise him in your first letter. Maybe he doesn't own one. Most speakers today don't wear them except at fancy banquets.

Rule 12. Pretalk cocktail parties are in order. They warm up the speaker, and the committee. But don't overspike his drinks thinking you are generous. Wait till the talk is over. Don't have him meet too many people. You'll tire him.

Rule 13. March into the banquet or luncheon. Don't straggle in like a bunch of carpenters going off job. Don't leave the speaker "on his own." Keep him in hand. It looks nicer to the audience.

Rule 14. Don't put the speaker next to the club's greatest talker. He'll wear the speaker down. Be friendly and considerate at the dinner, but not verbose.

Rule 15. Invocation at times is in order, at other times it is not. The same with singing patriotic songs. There is a time and place for everything.

Rule 16. Find out in advance what the speaker likes to eat. Maybe he doesn't like fish. Why make him eat it then? He's a guest in your "house." Maybe a club sandwich will do.

Rule 17. If steaks are served, find out how he likes them.

Why give him a rare one when he likes them well done? He is not your mother-in-law, but he can cuss you out just as much.

Rule 18. Pass the celery. Many a thoughtless chairman will leave it in front of him the entire meal, with the poor speaker just dying for something green to eat.

Rule 19. Pass the gravy. Many a speaker has had the gravy passed for his apple pie. Don't hog the biscuits. You can't expect the speaker to yell, "Pass the cream and sugar, you bums! !"

Rule 20. Don't overcrowd the speaker's table with all the past presidents, vice presidents and two-minute speakers. Give the speaker elbow room. He doesn't want somebody next to him always bumping his fork.

Rule 21. Avoid a lot of long-winded preliminaries that only two members want to hear. Keep that for the business meeting.

Rule 22. When you introduce people, ask the audience to "hold the applause." This will cut down on time and won't embarrass the fellow who gets little applause.

Rule 23. Start on time. Make this a habit, and your group will soon learn to be on time. If it is an evening meeting, have music played while people are assembling. It makes the auditorium cheerful, and people less restless.

Rule 24. Pay the speaker before his talk. Elbert Hubbert once said he always did this "so the speaker wouldn't worry during his speech whether he was going to be paid." Why pay a speaker five weeks later? He has just financed your meeting.

Rule 25. Be generous with expenses if this is part of your deal. Never give the speaker $9.20 for his expenses. Make it an even ten bucks. He'll repay you with *national* publicity.

Rule 26. If you are taking care of the speaker's suite, be sure the cashier knows about it, to avoid embarrassment when the speaker checks out and finds a cashier who says bluntly, "Nobody said nothing to me about paying your bill, mister."

Rule 27. Don't invite the speaker out to dinner, then bring along a flock of gabby wives to ogle the speaker. He has to be polite, but being polite is tiring. He can relax better with men. After the speech, of course, that's a different story.

Rule 28. Take the speaker to his train. Don't let him get a last-minute bad impression because all the boys were up in 202 having a good time and forgot the speaker.

Rule 29. If you visit with the speaker in his room, don't use his telephone unless you are sure the room is charged to the club or convention.

Rule 30. If you order things, such as soda pop, in the speaker's room, pay cash for them even if the room is charged; you don't want some treasurer to think the speaker threw a binge on the club's money.

Rule 31. If you do take a speaker out after his speech to

show him the sins or sights of the town, don't bring a lot of hens along, unless you have one for him. Spending night after night with a lot of wives, bores speakers stiff. Get him a companion. Don't be selfish.

Rule 32. Before or after the speech don't line the speaker up for a lot of handshakes. Spare the guy! Take him away from bores, and don't bring one along with you!

Rule 33. Don't ask the speaker a million questions such as "First time here?" ... "When did you arive?" ... "Where do you go next?" ... "Like traveling these days?" ... "Ever get nervous before a speech?" ... "How'd you get in business?"

Rule 34. Find out if you're having a drinking speaker, then don't assign some nondrinker to him. If he doesn't drink, don't assign the club's best bourbon tosser.

Rule 35. Don't let the speaking room get filled up with smoke. Open the windows. Call for ventilation. Don't expect the speaker to do this. He is too polite. He will just stand up in the smoke area and his speech will suffer.

Rule 36. Keep the place cool. Too many halls are cool until five hundred furnaces walk in and sit down, then the place heats up. Keep it cool so the speaker won't be sweated out. This kills more speeches than anything you can do to a speaker.

Rule 37. Don't overintroduce a speaker as the "man who as a child, who as a youth, who as a man. . . ." Don't over-build him. The audience expects only a human being with a nice speech; not a superman.

Rule 38. Don't underintroduce the speaker as "the man who needs no introduction." We all need introductions. Even the President of the United States. Tell enough of the man's background to whet the audience's appetite for the man's message.

Rule 39. Don't tell a lot of Pat and Mike jokes to introduce the speaker. One good joke is enough. Remember, you are to introduce the speaker, not give the speech.

Rule 40. Never "give" the speaker. Always "present" the speaker. It is in far better taste.

Rule 41. Tell the speaker how long you want him to speak; otherwise, a long-winded one will go on all night long or into your afternoon schedule.

Rule 42. Don't hire a speaker for so many minutes. Some of the best, and most expensive, speeches are the shortest.

Rule 43. If the meeting place is away from the speaker's hotel, assign somebody to drive him over and back. Don't put him on his own.

Rule 44. Don't leave the speaker on his own after his speech, but assign somebody to entertain him that night, or to see that he is happy.

Your speaker can be a booster for your club, meeting or convention; then again, he can tear you to the ground as he travels around the country meeting people.

Index